a picture is worth...

the voice of today's high school students

ARCH STREET PRESS
VALLEY FORGE, PA

CONTENTS

The *a picture is worth...* Program:

Amy Anselmo *Designer*
Alisa del Tufo *Executive Producer*
Janice Levy *Photographer*
•
David Castro *President & CEO, I-LEAD, Inc.*
Robert Rimm *Managing Editor*

a picture is worth...
Personal Stories, Photography and Essay Writing

a picture is worth... provides a standards-based, creative and dynamic high school curriculum component. It supports the Common Core State Standards, particularly those focused on writing and language. *a picture is worth...* successfully engages students, even those facing reading and writing challenges, in a process that strengthens communication skills, social awareness, reading and writing.

a picture is worth... offers youth the opportunity to find their voice, surface their values, and connect with others in creative and affirming ways. The project integrates academic skills such as **literacy**, the development of **critical thinking, communications, community engagement, photography** and **technology skills** with values of **integrity, self-awareness, empathy** and **leadership.**

a picture is worth... uses writing, audio stories and photography to create powerful interactive narratives; the curriculum offers a framework that engages students in crafting involving stories about their lives. The program is the result of a collaboration between I-LEAD, Threshold Collaborative, photographer Janice Levy and I-LEAD Charter School—its teachers, staff and learners.

The Story of Our Success:
Personal Stories and Narrative Essays
in Secondary Education

This work grew from the seed of a simple idea: to nurture the voice of young learners struggling to achieve in one of the most challenged educational systems in America. The program began in Reading, Pennsylvania, the site of I-LEAD Charter School (ILCS), with a mission to serve families seeking alternatives to the community's failing educational system.

In 2011, *The New York Times* recognized Reading's "unwelcome distinction." The city suffers the largest poverty rate of any in America; its families recognize the connection between their dire economic conditions and the collapse of educational achievement. The record shows local high school dropout rates exceeding 50%, with college-degree attainment lagging below 9%, pushing Reading's poverty rate up to a tragic 41%.

ILCS works toward community empowerment and equity in Reading's most challenged neighborhoods. The curriculum combines leadership education, character development and academic achievement, with a theory of change that believes when the youth of a community become educated, committed and effective, they can become productive and politically engaged change-makers, leading to breakthrough community transformations.

The improvement of writing skills has always been among secondary education's most important causes. ILCS maintains a special focus on narrative writing; helping students to master the art of reading and writing stories is an essential part of their social, emotional and academic learning. Competence in analyzing and composing narratives forms a critical part of the national Common Core educational standards.

Surfacing Voice and Crafting Stories

This is no surprise. Across all cultures and throughout recorded history, stories have served as the foundation for human understanding. Narratives provide a sort of DNA for human consciousness. In the hard sciences, we can think of theories as very precise stories that can be rigorously tested through experience. In the humanities, we constantly employ intricate narratives to understand the complexities of the world around us. Stories underlie all higher-order, systemic thought. In the words of Dr. Pamela Rutledge, Director of the Media Psychology Research Center, "Stories are how we think. They are how we make meaning of life. Call them schemas, scripts, cognitive maps, mental models, metaphors or narratives. Stories are how we explain how things work, how we make decisions, how we justify our decisions, how we persuade others, how we understand our place in the world, create our identities, and define and teach social values."

Mindful of the power of storytelling, ILCS's quest in this program is to assist students in creating a personal essay collection to engage them and provide relevant content for reflection, learning and action. ILCS wants to share stories from the heart that will inspire, while helping students in and beyond the Reading school—indeed nationally—improve their writing skills.

Critical Thinking

As learners, our love affair with stories be-gins as children when we project ourselves into the narratives we are told. Sometimes the stories that matter most come from books and mainstream media, but often they come from relatives and friends. Young learners have always developed their sense of self and community through sharing sto-ries. This collective story-sharing approach is at the core of ILCS's work. As we mature, we try to understand how our personal stories fit within the larger narratives that belong to our family, friends, community and even our society as a whole. We learn to see how our stories nest within one another like the countless rings of an ancient tree.

Our turbulent information age has made sto-ries even more potent, and our ability to vet them more essential. Thanks to the ubiquity of computers, smartphones and Internet connectivity, humans everywhere on earth have become massive producers and con-sumers of information. Societies that enjoy information-technology access spend each day swimming in vast oceans of words and digital images. Contemplate that the earth's entire surface has now been photographed, that the Internet currently contains more than 350 billion unique pictures, that Google's database includes more than 30 million fully scanned books, that humans are producing more than a billion Tweets per week....

Our ability to produce goods and services, to create value for one another, requires us to make sense of this data maelstrom, to select relevant patterns through the construction and critical analysis of the stories we employ as filters and organizing tools. It is only through such narrative structures that we can recognize, track, assess and predict trends. Through stories, we grapple with the enormous complexities of life as we engage in creative planning and strategic action toward desired outcomes and away from perceived troubles and dangers. The information age has exploded humanity's diversity of narrative, along with the raw material of experience it seeks to comprehend.

Story Becomes Essay

"Storytelling is an excellent way to bring out events of a child's upbringing through words, and to share his or her culture as a means of educating and instilling moral values."
Josephine Torres-Boykins
Learning Facilitator, I-LEAD Charter School

Against this backdrop, we can understand why it has never been more important for schools to help learners harness the power inherent in our stories—to **master the art of reading, analyzing and writing narrative essays, with special attention to personal narratives.** The narrative essay form is essential to modern life, as is the ability to think critically—to understand and express values and ideas succinctly. While students in secondary and higher education are often asked to read formal articles and books, the more limited format provided through the narrative essay serves as the most prevalent and important scale of writing in modern schools and organizations. At work within their communities and families, almost all students will be asked to write essays as they mature and take their place in the world.

Within the broader essay form, the *personal* essay is becoming increasingly critical to interpersonal success within organizations. In taking up the writer's identity, and relating his or her personality, strengths, shortcomings and values within the context of a unique story, the personal essay communicates something vital about its author's past, present and future, even if only implicitly; it often serves to link the individual's story to the larger narratives that create meaning within families, organizations, communities and society as a whole. Healthy communities depend upon the development of successful teams; individual members must have a deep sense not only of one another's strengths and weaknesses, but of their shared journey and the potential to aid one another's travels and travails. **The personal essay serves as an entry to productive collaboration within groups.** Through its many faces—the college application, cover letter, sales pitch, grant request, elevator speech, campaign speech and even marriage proposal—the evolving content of one's personal essay serves as the gateway to all relationships of importance: personal, spiritual, economic and political.

The personal essay also grapples with feelings and emotions, conveying vital ideas about values, motivation and matters of the heart. It thus plays a leading role in advancing social and emotional learning within organizational life. Whenever we are asked to introduce ourselves or to form new relationships, we revisit the core questions treated within a personal essay: Who am I? Why am I here? What do I want? How can I contribute? *a picture is worth...* addresses these practical and ineffable qualities in creative and powerful ways.

Clarity and Grammar

"We were able to emphasize good grammar and sentence structure because the students were very motivated to share their ideas and experiences so that other people would understand them. The students now know that their stories are not a liability but their strength. Learning to share them was very powerful and has given them courage to really be in their lives and identify their hopes."

Manuel Guzman
Learning Facilitator, I-LEAD Charter School

The lifelong work of improving writing skills requires that we master social conventions regarding language and expression. To practice the rules of grammar, punctuation and effective style strengthens our ability to communicate clearly, helping readers decode our writing and thereby gain access to our thoughts and feelings. A firm grasp of the formal rules may also liberate us, enabling choices that creatively depart from the norm. To understand parts of speech and technical construction of sentences is to uncover mysteries about the expression of thought and emotion that remain useful throughout our lives. Where the essays included in this work have departed from the local rules, the writers have done so intentionally and with respect for them.

The Role of Voice

Good writing requires more than adherence to .grammatical and stylistic conventions. Particularly within the personal essay form, good writing demonstrates *voice*. This project honors that powerful insight through the use of spoken personal narrative. Starting with the story of each learner, this curriculum grows from an interview that happens early in the semester; beginning with each student's voice, this project grounds itself in the essential strength of the spoken word as a harbinger of awareness, creativity and human connection. By telling their story to an interviewer, preserving it as a recording, listening to and sharing it, students begin to connect their experiences with those of others, building powerful opportunities for empathy and action.

As the poet Maya Angelou said, "Words mean more than what is set down on paper. It takes the human voice to infuse them with deeper meaning." The art of writing invites us to select words and craft expressions conveying personality, perspective, desire, pathos, irony, humor and emotion. The personal essay provides perhaps the most immediate and direct opportunity to develop voice. Voice reminds us that there is no information, knowledge, understanding, meaning or action without the presence of a living soul with hopes, fears and frailties. In some circles within Western culture, efforts have been underway to teach students to speak and write with a kind of objective voice that strives to negate its deeply personal reality—as if what is communicated could attempt to stand above or beyond particular human existence. Voice reveals that all truth entails observation and perspective, in this sense bound by the observer's narrative context. The essays included here celebrate that voice.

Social Context

Challenged communities live not through abstract social statistics, but through real individuals and families, human beings with souls surviving and often thriving in the face of poverty, hopelessness, oppression, discrimination and violence. Because of our unique experiences, we see the world and describe it through a different set of stories. We draw meaning and understanding from narratives that differ in important ways from mainstream literary content and educational networks. This work seeks to shine a light upon and amplify these alternative stories— strong and beautiful examples of the personal essay form—to serve learners growing up, facing obstacles and succeeding within settings that share departures from the norm.

By sharing these stories brought to life through the faces and voices of our young learners, ILCS expects to inspire new learning and new educational pathways for their peers. In studying the personal narrative essay, we must question why it should be necessary to reach far away—to places remote in time and culture—for strong examples of the essay form. We can make a different choice that contributes highly relevant and engaging content to present school curricula. Powerful stories, shining examples of the personal essay, arise *within* challenged communities; they spring from the minds and hearts of the learners themselves. We know why. Art and genius beat in every human heart.

Please visit www.apictureisworth.org for details on implementing a full model curriculum for *a picture is worth....* There you will also find additional photos, blogs and audio segments produced by the students who participated in our inaugural program.

David Castro, Ashoka Fellow
President and CEO, I-LEAD, Inc.

Alisa del Tufo, Ashoka Fellow
Executive Director, Threshold Collaborative

a picture is worth...

Audio Linked QR Codes

At the end of each essay is a QR code that links to audio interviews conducted by Threshold Collaborative with students from I-LEAD Charter School.

Listen to these interviews on SoundCloud; you can access them on your computer with the URLs listed or by scanning the code with your mobile device. (You may need to download a barcode reader app, such as "Red Laser" or "QR Reader.")

Enjoy this unique multimedia approach to storytelling!

listen

The Girl Who Found Her Way

My name is Aaliya Bonas. I am 15 years of age and my family members are the most important, crazy people in my life. My mom is funny, smart and strict. My dad is what you can say awesome, talented and good at music. I have 25 brothers and sisters so I can't tell you all about them, but you will know some of them later on.

I grew up in a rough home. My stepmom would always beat me for no reason. She would often lie to my dad and tell him that I would get in trouble and curse at her. I hated her for that, and also her family would come and sleep on my bed and put my brother and me on the hard cold floor. Sometimes I wished my dad would see what really happened, but he was so busy being in love with her that he lost focus on his own kids. People tried to tell him yet he didn't listen. But other than that my life was fine; school was great, the education wonderful and easy to learn and understand. People in the school were very kind to me, but not to my brother. I had to fight for him every day. It was so bad that my dad wanted to send me away for that.

After a while I got tired of being there so I called my mom and asked her if I can live with her in the USA. My mom said yes. I was so happy when she did. I couldn't wait to tell my brother the good news, but to my surprise he was very sad and didn't want me to leave at all. I didn't know how to tell him I was leaving the next day, so I left without saying anything. I got to the airport and my face lit up like a Christmas tree. I saw my mom for the first time; the expression was happy and exciting. I wanted to try everything and anything in the food court. I heard the food was everything and more so I was excited to try it there. I had Burger King for the first time and it was so good I didn't want to stop eating it. After my feast, we headed to my new home. I was happy I had my own room and thought life couldn't get better than that, until I got everything I wanted. I couldn't ask for more, life was good and I had a new start.

I would often call my brother and father to express my feelings to them. My brother would often cry on the phone but I would tell him to be strong and wait because I would be home to visit soon. I started feeling sad after a while because my brother wasn't there with me. I had a strong relationship with him; he was like my everything.

I would often try to tell my mom that I wanted to go back home. I miss my home there so much I would cry myself to sleep at night. My mom wouldn't listen to me so I started acting bad in school and home and pretty much everywhere that I went with her. Then I had asked to go to a party one day. She did say yes but I didn't come home that night. I spent the whole night out and got home the next day. My mom and I fought that day, and Children and Youth Services had to come to my house. After like two months my mom and I started going downhill. We would fight all the time, scream at each other, just do everything to basically hurt one another. I got tired of the fighting and screaming so I told her just to send me back home because fighting wouldn't solve anything. My mom said she would if only she had the money but that was a lie because she did have the money, but she would spend it on drinks or fast food. It hurt me to know that my mom would keep me here to be unhappy. It's like I had to be in jail. I would often cry and try to call my dad and tell him what's going on. He did send for me but my mom didn't let me go. It was difficult to be there now be-cause I didn't want to be there and she wasn't letting me go anywhere, so I would go back to my bad ways.

Now the fighting and screaming was worse. We would curse at each other and at my younger brother and sister. Then we had counseling. They would come to my house and have long conversations about working together to build a relationship with my mom. I was beyond angry. It was her fault that I was not able to go back home and be with my family. Counseling failed because I was not paying any attention to them or trying to build a relationship with my mom. She would keep me in the house, tell me I couldn't go anywhere and come straight home from school. I got tired of that and changed my ways. I started being nice to her and was treating my little brother and sister with respect and kindness. Sometimes we would have our ups and downs but I was kind of thinking about what did the good do and what did the bad do. They evened out but my mom and I were still fighting even though I was good or bad so I just kept with my bad ways. The fighting I didn't care about anymore. The way we were I didn't care about at all; I just stayed the way I was and she the way she was.

Life was just horrible and I didn't care, then I came up with the idea to make a Facebook page, without my mom knowing. I knew that if she found out she would get angry but I didn't care so I did anyway. I started adding all kinds of different men on there and of course my people from back home so we could talk and laugh about the times we had when

I was home. My mom would make me feel like crap, like nobody wanted me or nobody would marry me when I got older. So the Facebook I made was so that men would like my photos and tell me that I was beautiful and pretty. I would be on Facebook every day. I loved the attention, the love from other people, and the kind of comments I would get just made me hungry for more, until the day my mom found my Facebook page. She was very angry and took my phone away, but I was all caught up in the feeling of the Facebook people loving me and showing me that I am special, so I made another one. People might tell me that I look pretty and awesome but the words my mom told me stick with me all the time. It's like I don't believe people when they tell me I am beautiful. I feel like nothing, I am nothing; I am useless and just about crap. Men would talk to me on the streets and I would talk to them. I knew they only wanted sex but I didn't care. I didn't give them sex but we did talk and some other rated-R stuff.

My dream from then on was to become a stripper. I knew I would love the job because of the way I was treated and the life I lived. I am a very good dancer and stripping I thought would be a good thing for me, because there was a lot of money and dancing of course. I didn't tell my mom what I want to be because I don't want to have her in my life anymore. The fighting did stop and we were not really talking to each other, and it went on like that for a while. Now I have reached the time in my life that we are talking but not really in the relationship zone.

I am going back to my lovely country Trinidad and Tobago, and I will reunite with my brother. Life in America is not always what you think it is; you just got to come and find out for yourself. Now I am going home in a month. I am excited and ready to get the life that I want and deserve. So if it's anything I got to tell the people who are reading this: Don't be what people want you to be, be what you want to be and be good and success-ful at it.

I have learned a lot from being in this country. I learned that you can't always get what you want and you have to work hard for everything you want. I also have a relationship with my stepdad but we often fight or argue with each other. That happens because of my mom, as she tends to make us get heated with each other. Again my mom has a lot to do with my life and a lot with messing it up. Sometimes I wish that shit would be good but that will never happen so forget it. I lost hope at this point. I started smoking, drinking and doing everything that would upset her. I didn't care about what she had to say anymore.

My life went down hill from there, the fighting got worse, and the cursing and screaming did as well. I did badly in school, cursing at teachers, skipping classes, coming home late. My mom lied about me going back to Trinidad. I became sad and upset, so I turned back to Facebook. I was talking to a boy who my friend had hooked me up with. I did really like him, and I thought that he really liked me the same way. So when we started talking he had asked me to send him pictures of myself naked. I did refuse at first but then I sent them anyway. He said that he would not show anybody and I did believe him. After about a month we stopped talking and so did my friend and I. We hated each other and shit just got worse. So about two weeks into not talking, I was with my stepdad when my mom called him and showed him the pictures that I sent to my ex-boyfriend.

I thought my life was over. As soon as I got home, I ran upstairs and started popping pills. I wanted to die, but my little brother came and found me in time. I went to the hospital. They said that I needed to stay there for a while. When I was in there, I learned that life is important and you have to make the best of it. When I got out I switched schools. I was ready to make a change in my life for the better. My mom loved the idea of that but I didn't. It would be hard making new friends and starting over, but I was ready for it anyway.

So I got to the new school and was already depressed and upset in being there. I was not doing my work or anything for that matter. My mom got upset and said she would send me to my brother's house. I didn't care about what she had to say. I was at that point where I was ready to die and life wasn't what I wanted. So I came to school and was not doing anything. Teachers were upset about that, so I had the school call my mom and tell her to check me out of school. She refused to. I knew she would do that so I just stayed and waited for time to pass. I went to New York that weekend and my dad did call me. That's when I remembered why I went to school, why I wanted to be somebody and become someone.

So I am back in school doing my work and everything that I am supposed to. My mom and I are on the same page as far as talking to each other but not building a relationship. We both want to stay where we are right now and, as for my life, school's great, home is okay I guess and everything is where it's supposed to be. My plan for the future is to become a nurse in the army and support my family and those who are close to me who need help. As for the way my mom treated me, I will never treat my children that way. So a little info for the people who are reading this: It doesn't matter if you don't want to be around or like your mom 'cause she is your mom at the end of the day. Plus life will not always be fair. You just have to make it fair on your own.

I am Aaliyah Bonas

soundcloud.com/a-picture-is-worth/aaliyah

My Life Story in Never-Ending Words!

In the following essay, I will be writing about my family, my community and myself. My family comes from Ponce, Puerto Rico, a small, relatively unknown city. My father gave my name to me, because I came out light-skinned like my mother but then when I turned a month old my complexion fully changed. The meaning of my name is unique in Spanish and means light. So when I walk in a room I feel like I shine. I grew up without a father figure; my mom and dad split up shortly after I was born. I always blamed myself for this, but then as I grew older I realized that both had gone in different directions. I could no longer blame myself for something I had not done.

My third-to-oldest sister and I have always had a feud, not that I encourage it but I guess there is jealousy coming from her side being that I was last born. So one day my mom had gone to the bodega and left me with my sister. I was 7 years old and she would always beat on me. I was tired of the abuse, so I hid behind her bedroom door with a pen in my hand and when she came in I stabbed her neck. She ran off and told my aunt who was babysitting us, and that day I got a spanking. My sister and I still do not get along as I would like, but there is no longer abuse.

I can remember this like it was yesterday: I was 9 years old and it was Christmas, so mami sent me off to bed and told me that if I didn't listen, Santa would not bring me my present. I rushed off to my room and pretended to go to sleep. In the middle of the night, I got up and saw mami wrapping Christmas presents and started to cry; I then knew that there was no Santa and was upset. Then she explained to me that Santa was once real, but he had gone on to a better life and that she was his special helper.

My sister, the one I previously mentioned, has an ugly greed for money. She is known as the hungry activist. Growing up, I have seen her actions and behavior that are not proper. Me, I'm a wonderful, loving person but sometimes I tend to slack, so therefore I am the slacker. I'm 18 years old at this point so I am legal, although in my family, when you move out that is when you are legal.

I met this boy in school and oh was he a handsome young man. I was head over heels for him so I got to know him and we exchanged numbers. Unlike most guys, he told me that he wanted to meet my mother. I warned him and explained that mami was a tough cookie, but he insisted. I invited him over to my house and told mami to please not embarrass my friend or me. That day went better than I expected; she was friendly, loving and charming towards him. I thought I was dreaming.

The hardest thing I have done to date would be raising my child. Kids are a handful, especially when you are a single parent. It is not a walk in the park. When I was 18, the handsome young boy and I really hit it off. We became a couple and shortly after a year we conceived a child. I was scared to tell my mother that I was pregnant, but it was something that had to be done. She was upset at the beginning but a child is a blessing and she supported me one hundred percent. As months went by, my belly started to grow and I felt the life that was growing inside of me. I told my boyfriend that he had to tell his mother and so he did. Now I am four months pregnant.

During a normal day for me, or at least I thought it was, my mom came into my room and told me to get ready to go out to eat with my other sister. I found that strange. So I got dolled up and off we went. I noticed that my mom had a small appetite and really was not eating. After that, we drove to a park nearby and I saw that my mom walked off, sat on a bench and started to cry. I asked my sister what's wrong with mami. I stood up to run to her and my sister grabbed me, trying to calm me down. She told me that there was nothing wrong with mami. So I'm like, all right, what is going on? She told me that it was Anthony (that was the name of the handsome boy). My heart dropped when she told me the tragedy that occurred. She told me that he was no longer with us. I didn't know how to react or what to say. I busted down into tears and could not believe it. I called his mother and begged her to tell me that it wasn't true, if this was a bad joke, but no, it was true. The father of my child would not be there to see his seed be born or grow physically. I gave birth to my child; he was so beautiful and my motherhood instincts came right away.

I attended Reading High School and my senior year was very difficult. I had a lot of absences and was not doing as well as I should have been doing. One day in late March, my counselor called me into the office and told me that I would not be graduating that year, so I told him to withdraw me. After I dropped out, I began working at Ashley's Furniture, which was hell but I knew that I had to do it; I'm a single mother and had to work. I didn't last very long at that job, maybe about two months. Then I fell into a great depression when my child was 5 months old. I couldn't get out of bed, hardly ate and was a mess. Mom was not having it. She told me to get my butt up and to do something with my life. After a year I began working at a family diner but I knew that I did not want to bus tables forever so I quit from the job.

So I'm at square one again and I think to myself that my biggest mistake was not getting pregnant at a young age but dropping out of school. A couple of friends had told me that a new school was opening up and that it was a great opportunity for me. One day I got up and decided to go into the school and apply. I got accepted. Even though I was 20 years old, I got an opportunity to receive my diploma at the I-LEAD Charter School. So at that moment I felt such a relief, as if I had an angel on my shoulder all along. That is what I really want: to receive my diploma, to finish my senior year and know to myself that I can reach that goal. Now I'm attending school and doing a really good job, going to school full time then coming home and taking care of my child.

Everything was going great and the summer, too. When the school year came about, I began to slack—not because I wanted to but my body started to feel differently. I felt like this for quite a while but did not know what was happening to me. So by April of the school year, the teachers told me that I needed to catch up on my work. I did not want to give up, I really didn't, but a part of me did. One day, I could not get out of bed, missed school for a couple of days straight and was rushed to the emergency room, where I was diagnosed with a disease. I was living with and did not even know about it. But now it made sense why I was not feeling well. I felt so overwhelmed when I found out that I have Lupus, a disease that takes over the immune system. So now I have to live with this disease. The school year is almost over and there is all this work to be made up, but I was given another chance to make up what I missed. My day of triumph and hard work will pay off. I am such a grateful person and I truly appreciate this chance that I am given. I will live up to it. It is not easy waking up and sometimes I cannot move, but I look up and I thank God. I thank him because I am alive and I have a beautiful son and family, and friends and wonderful people who support me. I will not give up!

My strongest trait is strength. Yes, I am a strong, independent woman who will take all obstacles thrown at me as challenges to knock every one of them down. What makes me happy is to be able to wake up every day and watch my son grow into a beautiful boy. He has such manners for his age. I know that I am raising him the best way that I can, and that his father is in heaven looking down on his boy. I thank God and all of those individuals who have supported me throughout these tough years and have given me a positive aspect on life. This is my life story in never-ending words; I say it that way because my journey con-  tinues from here, so it is not a goodbye from me; it's a see you later. God bless y como decimos los hispanos hasta luego.

I am Lucy Casimiro

soundcloud.com/a-picture-is-worth/lucy

Family, Hopefulness, Ashley

I always knew that my family wasn't normal or perfect. Even when I was little I knew we weren't a typical family. We lived in Brooklyn, New York, in a big green building. My family's apartment was on the first floor, the last door on the left. I remember my room. I had a big princess bed. I rarely remember those times, but I do remember when we moved. Every day before that I would say goodbye to my house, but I didn't know that it would be for good this time.

When my family and I moved to Reading, we moved into the greatest house in the world! It was beautiful. However, my family wasn't yet whole. My father was still a construction worker in Brooklyn and we only saw him on Sundays, sometimes Saturdays. I never thought much of it, until one day when I told my friend about it, she said that if she were only able to see her dad one day a week, that would make her too sad. But I continued to push it to the side. Eventually my dad stood for good. I don't remember why, or what job he got, but he was finally here and we were finally a whole family.

Everything was perfect for a while, but after a few years my family decided to move to Florida. First, though, my brothers and I had to live with my grandmother in New York. That sucked. I was in third grade attending P.S 198 and my class hated me. For a whole year I had books thrown at me, was cursed out by other students, bullied and secluded. Even my teacher, Ms. Perrera, made that year terrible. I worked so hard all the time, but all she could do was criticize and tell me that my work wasn't good enough. She lost all my work and told me that I never turned it in, even when she collected it right out of my hand or when my mother would personally hand it to her! I had no one to turn to, no friends, no teachers. I couldn't talk to my grandmother, my parents were barely around and my brothers didn't understand. I just wanted to disappear. I would have dreams of running away. I would even pack my stuff in hopes that one night I would finally have the courage to do it. But I never did.

Eventually I just stopped going and told everyone that I moved to Florida. If people saw me in the street I told them that I was just visiting. I didn't want anyone from that hell of a school to know that I was still around. Then finally the day came and we were out to Florida. I was so excited that I was finally going to leave hell.

Initially we moved to help my grandmother with her home because a hurricane broke her roof. Living with her was terrible. She was a grumpy old hag who had a nasty farm with a million chickens. School, however, was so much better than in New York. I had friends and people didn't bully me, and nobody lived in my neighborhood because the houses are so far from the school that everyone had to take a bus. I was finally happy in school for the first time since second grade.

Fortunately our time was up and my family and I moved back to Reading. I was finally back in my old house, in my old room. That house had so many great memories. It was my family's first actual house and not an apartment, the first house I ever got to paint the walls of, the first house with a room for everyone, and the first house we moved into when we left Brooklyn and came to Reading. But most important was my old school. I loved 12th and Marion. I was there since kindergarten, and now I would be graduating as a fifth grader. School was so amazing. I looked forward to going everyday and learning something new, just excited that it was my last year of elementary school.

Finally! I am a sixth grader. Ha ha, back then I felt so grown, and when I look back now I only realize how much of a child I really was, how my mentality was so immature, how much others' mentalities were just as bad as mine. Because of that my sixth-grade year sucked! By that time in people's lives, they felt as if they were adults. How you did your hair was a factor to how popular you were. What shoes you wore became more important than learning. School was just a place to hang out with your friends. To me, school was a place to learn. I was never worried about my hair or the shoes I wore, and that was the reason I had no friends except one, my best friend Marcus Miranda. He was the only person who really understood me and I really appreciated that. Having only one friend through school is just terrible, though.

I remember there was one boy who really did not like me. All he did all day was call me names, and hit and threaten me, like he had nothing better to do. It felt like he came to school to bully me. He was the reason I became depressed, but whether I was or not didn't seem to matter. I dreaded going to school every day. I hated having every class with him. I hated that nobody noticed how depressed I was. Thank goodness I was moving again.

Unlike the different house I lived in, my depression stayed the same. The new house that I lived in, however, only made it worse. For the rest of that year I lived with constant fights at home, more bullying in school, and again I lived in a house with 11 people with no one to talk to.

For the next two years I moved and moved again, but still continued to live with this depression. Different houses, different streets, different schools, same depression. I was living while trying to push it all to the side. I overcame it sometimes, but other days I would feel like the world hated me. I questioned my faith, and then just decided not to believe in God anymore. I didn't believe in anything anymore.

I was simply a shell in my own life: looking pleasant on the outside but empty inside. All I wanted was for someone to come up to me and tell me that they knew exactly what I was going through and how I felt. I wanted them to tell me that they had a solution, but that didn't happen. Why didn't anybody just ask me how I was or how I felt? Nobody cared, and that killed me. Thirteen years old and alone. Sure I was in a room full of people, but people who were blind to the truth. But who can blame them? I couldn't expect my mom and dad to understand every feeling I had or every thought that was running through my head. At that point, sticking to myself was the only option.

Eventually the word "crazy" began to be thrown at me a lot. So one night I decided to carve the word into my arm, scarring it there just like it was in my heart. For some strange reason the pain felt amazing. It was the only thing I've felt in a long time. I was scared of the judgment that would come from others, so long sleeves were now a necessity.

Cutting myself was scary, and I never thought I would do it again. Nobody knew and that made it so much easier. I was a loner in school, so questioning my cuts never happened.

But then my wish came true and someone finally noticed how sad I always was, and told one of my guidance counselors to check up on me. Her sweet voice and sense of understanding just made me open up with everything. My depression, my cutting, my sadness, everything I could possibly think of.

Worst decision of my life.

This woman decided that I was not only a threat to myself but to others as well. She even made the insinuation that I was suicidal. She wouldn't let me leave school and even called my mother and told her everything. Just when I thought I had someone to trust, someone in a matter of minutes proved me wrong.

The hour that I waited for my mom felt more like 100. I could only imagine how she felt. Was she mad at me? Was she going to hit me? What was she going to say to me? She came, and when my guidance counselor pulled her into the room and closed the door, a million thoughts ran through my mind. I could only imagine what they were saying. Next thing I knew, the doors opened and I was told that I was getting admitted into a psycho ward. This only made the feeling of being crazy more realistic than ever.

Being at the hospital was terrible. I was locked in an all-white room with one bed in the middle, while my mom sat in the hall. We were there for hours. Finally when one of the doctors left the room, I caught the door with my foot and just stared at my mom. Nothing but eye-to-eye contact. Then I finally managed to cough up some words. "Are you mad at me?" That was all I could say. So many words and all I could worry about was whether or not my mom was mad at me or not. Her reply was, "What do you think?" Without another word, I looked at the ground and went back into my room and started to cry.

After my mom and I were questioned for hours, we were finally given the opportunity to go home. The ride home was silent and awkward. Arriving there was the complete opposite. Judgment and rude remarks were getting yelled at me from every direction. I had to get away so I ran to my room and sat in the dark. When I was called down for dinner, I didn't go. When it was time for school, I woke up extra early so no one would have to confront anyone. Ever.

A long period of time passed and finally things got so much easier. Eighth grade was a good year. I made friends and hung out with people. Nobody bullied me. I wasn't popular, but I wasn't a loner either and that was OK for me. That year went by so fast.

Next thing I knew it was summertime and going out to the park with my friends. I had a cellphone and it was awesome. And then we were moving again. The move came at the perfect moment because now I was in high school and had met this amazing guy. He made me feel so special and I was so happy to be with him. He made me feel so beautiful; all of my insecurities were gone. My parents and I finally started to get along. The depression faded away. I never felt the need to cut anymore and I lived in the best house ever. It was big and beautiful. The neighborhood I lived in was full of friendly people. Everything finally fell into place, and I was happy.

My best friend lived around the corner from me and we were in the same high school, so we hung out all the time. For the first time in a long time, I was happy just being myself.

And I've now come to realize that things always get better. Everyone has to go through hard times, some harder than others, but in time cloudy skies will clear away.

I am Ashley Chamorro

soundcloud.com/a-picture-is-worth/ashley

Take a Walk in My Shoes

My name is Jahida Marie Dejesus. Yes, I love my name. It's uncommon. I am 16 years old, born September 18th and raised in Reading, PA. My strongest qualities are dancing, listening and standing up for what I believe. I haven't really been to many places—Baltimore, Atlantic City, Wildwood and Washington, D.C.

I have two younger siblings, a brother and a sister. My brother Christian is 15 and my sister Viviana is 13. I had an older sister who passed away before I was born. I sometimes wish that I was the only child, because I could get more stuff and there would be fewer problems. But since I do have my brother and sister, I wouldn't change that for anything.

My mom and dad are not together; he has not been there since I was born. It makes me hate him for what he has done. It doesn't bother me that my mom and dad aren't together, but makes me mad that he couldn't be man enough to be in my life. My mom left him when she was about to give birth because he didn't want to go the hospital with her. So she said, "When I get back I'm packing my stuff and leaving." He would sell my baby stuff that people would give to my mom for me before I was born, for drugs. How sad is he for doing that! That's just so sad that he would go that low for drugs. I guess that's what people on drugs do to get what they need. But he never fixed it by trying to be in my life. So I couldn't care less about him. He's nothing to me.

Something that makes me happy is dance; it's what I do. I've been dancing since I was little. I have a passion for dance. It's a way for me to express myself, a stress relief and a way to have fun. I love to dance in front of people on stage. I don't get nervous, 'cause I just love the feeling of everyone watching and cheering me on. Their cheering shows they like how I dance and can tell I have a passion for it. It's not something I do 'cause I'm good at it, but because it makes me happy and is something I just love doing.

I love to help people learn dances because if I can, I'm more than happy to
help. I love helping people out if I can. I
don't care if they look so bad dancing, as
long as they're trying I don't mind going
over it a million times. But if they can
dance and don't try, then don't waste my
time. That's when I start to get mad and
don't want to help as much 'cause they
put in no effort.

I recently moved to the south side. I
hate it. It's so far from everything I did
and everyone I know. It's so boring.
There is nothing much I can do to keep
busy. There are not many kids my age to
hang with and it's so far from school. I'd
rather not live here. But I gotta admit it
feels much safer than my old house. It
was bad where I used to live and there
were shootings all the time. That's when
my brother got shot. After that, I felt so
unsafe. I didn't want to walk home from
school, I didn't wanna be anywhere
alone. I felt like my family was in dan-
ger, that those people might come after
us too because I know they knew who
we are and where we'd be. You know
how hard it was to see my little brother
in that hospital, helpless with cuts and
bruises, with all those wires and tubes on
him. But he lived and that's all that really
matters. That's a big reason why we
moved, and we also needed more
room.

I chose to come to I-LEAD instead of Reading High because I felt that I'd be better off here, and that I'd get a better education. It's smaller and more controlled, which means the class will not be all crazy with everyone doing whatever they want. Also there would not be fighting in class, with less drama. At Reading High, there'd be a fight every day and the classes have no control. If I would have gone there, I know I would have been too distracted, and got none of my work done and had bad grades. Plus with all the bad things going on, I probably would have got caught up in stuff that was not needed. The only thing I can think of that I missed out on when coming here is the sports. I did track, basketball and volleyball. I love sports; it's what I'm good at, like I could have gotten a scholarship from sports, but I chose to give that up to go here. Sometimes I question myself if that was what I should have done, but it turned out good 'cause I have As and Bs. So minus the sports thing, I like it here.

In my future, I'm really not sure what I am going to do. 'Cause I don't have much planned since all that can change. But I'd like to be a dance choreographer and also work with kids. As long as I am happy with my job, the money is not the most important if I'm doing what I love. I want to be a choreographer because I love to dance and teach, so why not get paid for doing something that I already know how to do and love? I want to work with kids because I love them and think we work very well together. I also have a very energetic kid-like personality.

I want to get married but have very high standards about that. I'd like to have two kids, a boy and a girl. I wish I can have twins but I don't think that will happen. I want to move out of this city when I'm  older, not too far just far enough that I can be away from all that craziness but close enough that I can always go back home....

I am Jahida Dejesus

soundcloud.com/a-picture-is-worth/jahida

A Glimpse of Life Through My Eyes

My family is full of crazy, fun, annoying and loving people. Most of the grown-ups in my family were born in the Dominican Republic, though all of their kids were born in the United States. The only children in my family who were probably born in the Dominican Republic are my two older brothers and everyone else whose parents never came to the United States. Most of my father's side of the family still lives in the Dominican Republic. Only some of his 18 brothers and sisters, my aunts and uncles, came to live in the United States with him. On the other hand, most of my mother's side of the family came to America when my mom was only 12. They are spread out all over the United States. A good amount of them live in New York, but I have family in Florida, Pennsylvania and Georgia, too.

I currently live with both of my parents, even though I am only supposed to be living with my mother, because that is what it says on our lease. I have three sisters but I only live with two of them. My oldest sister is Janelly, currently 17 years old. My other sister is Stephanie. I call her Phania. She is the middle sister. I am the youngest girl living in the house, for now. My youngest sister is Ashley. Unfortunately, I have not yet had the pleasure to meet her since she does not live with me and she also isn't my mother's daughter. From what I have seen in pictures, she is extremely pretty. She has green eyes and dirty blonde hair.

I have three brothers but I only live with one of them. He is my youngest brother, but I also find him the most annoying. We barely get along. We are always arguing and sometimes we do fight but then I just end up getting in trouble. His name is Javier but everyone calls him Javielito or baby. Javielito is nine right now but he still acts like he is four. My two other brothers are Brian and Javier. Brian is the oldest out of all the kids but he is my dad's son, not my mom's. Javier comes second in line after Brian but he isn't my mother's son either. The only reason I have two brothers named Javier is because their mothers named them after my father. Brian lives in Pennsylvania, which is where we are living at the moment. I get to see Brian all the time but since Javier lives in New Jersey I don't get to see him as often as I would like. I miss him like crazy.

The only other person who lives with me is my grandma. She has schizophrenia and diabetes. She is extremely sick but doesn't like taking her medicine. I feel that she doesn't really like me and I definitely know that she doesn't like Phania. She thinks Phania took her youth from her but that's only because she is sick. Even though she gets on my nerves often, I still love her. I know that she can't help that she is sick but it does get extremely annoying at times. If anything ever happened to her, though, I wouldn't know what I would do.

I consider my parents as the type of people who worry too much. They are extremely overprotective and it can get overwhelming sometimes. They are Dominican and can be very strict. My dad is the one who really doesn't let us do anything. When we want to go out with our friends or to a party, my sisters and I don't feel like we are trusted because most of the time he says no. I remember this one time I spent a few days hanging out with my boyfriend. I always came home early and it wasn't like I was spending the nights at his house. My dad ended up calling me while I was walking home from McDonald's with my boyfriend and his friend. He told me that I had to get home right away and he didn't want to tell me why. I went home and my boyfriend came with me. When I got home, my dad told me that I was grounded and that I was not allowed to go outside except when I had to go to school until he said I could. The reason he grounded me was that I spent the whole week outside on the streets and wasn't spending enough time home. You could imagine my surprise when I heard this, especially since I had only been spending a few days outside. I was so furious because that was the first time he had ever grounded me. My sisters were allowed to be out all they wanted, even though they were out all the time. I thought it was so unfair that I didn't even want to speak to my dad. That's the type of person he is and, like I said before, it can be extremely overwhelming. I still love him, though. He's my dad, and I would hate it if he didn't worry about us the way he does.

My mom is an amazing person. Her name is Yolanda Beatriz Gomez. Her maiden name was Rodriguez but when she got married she decided to change it. I don't know how she deals with everything she has been and is going through.

My dad and she have many problems. I think he loves her but his actions don't show it. I think my mom was in love with him at one point in her life, but now I just think she loves him because he has been such a big part of her life. She isn't in love with him anymore. When I was younger, I thought they had the perfect relationship and nothing was ever wrong between them. As I grew older, I realized that I was completely wrong. My dad has cheated on my mom before. My mom knows this but she still stays with him. I think she stays with him for us, her kids. If she could leave him and support us on her own I'm sure she would. We think my dad is cheating on her now, but he doesn't know we know. I love both of my parents more than anything in the world. I just don't feel they should be together. My mom deserves the best and my dad deserves someone who can teach him what being in love should really be like. Maybe he wouldn't cheat on her.

I live in Exeter, Pennsylvania. I've been living here for about five months now. I don't really know a lot about where I live now, but I do know that it is nothing like the place that I used to live, in Reading, Pennsylvania. Around where I live in Exeter it is quiet and there is never any trouble. In the winter you never see anyone outside and in the summer you barely see any kids out. It seems as if everyone is always in their houses or at the park but they are never outside of their houses in the front yard playing. It seems like a good place to live but it also feels so secluded from everything. To get from one place to another, you always have to drive because everything is so far. There are no parks that are close by and there definitely aren't any grocery stores nearby either. The only time someone would probably have fun around where I live would be in the park with a lot of family members or if you have a barbeque in your backyard. Other than that, there's really nothing to do. This would be the kind of place where I would want my daughter to grow up because I know it's safe for her as long as I keep my eye on her.

In Reading, it is completely different. It's more fun but also more dangerous. I moved to Reading from New York just as I was about to start the fifth grade. I remember I was so happy back then because we would finally be able to live in an actual house and not an apartment. Reading was a new setting for me. In New York I was never allowed to go out because my parents thought it was too dangerous. In Reading, though, I was allowed to go out with my friends and my sisters and it was completely fine with my parents. I would be out until my parents would tell me to come home, so I was never really out that late, except for when I went to parties. Then my parents let me stay out until about 1 a.m. I never thought that was long enough, so my sisters and I would always sneak back out and stay out until maybe 4 or 5 in the morning and come back home before my parents woke up.

Reading might be fun but it is also extremely dangerous. You would always hear about someone getting jumped, robbed, into fights and sometimes even getting killed. It was dangerous to walk around Reading by yourself in the night, but it could also be dangerous to walk around in the day. You never knew if you had something somebody else wanted or if you were going to be robbed at any moment. That's why I barely ever walked by myself when going anywhere. I always walked with either one of my sisters or I would tell one of my friends to come with me. I remember this one time there was a fight outside of my house. Two of my neighbors were fighting and I just thought that that fight was so completely pointless, especially because I remember at one point they actually used to be friends. It was between a Dominican guy and some other guy who was some type of white. I can remember thinking to myself that that Dominican guy can really fight. He beat the white guy up as if there was no effort put into it.

If I were not pregnant I would definitely still like to live in Reading rather than Exeter. I find Reading exciting and fun compared to Exeter. There is so much more to do. You can actually walk to anywhere you want to go in Reading. There's a corner store on almost every corner and it isn't difficult to get from one place to another by foot. Although I would rather live in Reading, I definitely think Exeter is the better place to raise my daughter. I wouldn't have to worry about her life every time she walked out of the house. There are plenty of kids who she can play with at the park and she will be in a safer environment. The only thing that I would most likely worry about would be racism. Even though some people don't like to admit it, racism is still out there. In Exeter there are mostly white people. You see the occasional Hispanic or African American, but the majority of people who live around me are Caucasian. Some of them might be racist and I don't want my daughter to grow up feeling bad about who she is and where she comes from. My daughter will be 50 percent Dominican, 25 percent Trinidadian, and 25 percent Caucasian. I know that her Dominican and Trinidadian sides will mostly show and I don't want her to ever be ashamed of what she is.

I was born on December 3, 1997, in Manhattan, New York, at the Metropolitan Hospital Center. I am currently 15 years old and my birthday isn't for another seven months. I live in Exeter now with my parents, two of my sisters, one of my brothers and my grandma. I don't fit in. I don't really communicate with them or speak to them as much as I would like to or as much as they do to each other. I have felt like I never really fit in with my family for a long time. Even when I was little I felt like this. At one point I remember thinking that I was adopted. That notion quickly went out the window when I realized I look too much like my father's side of the family and too much like my sister's to ever be adopted. I wasn't disappointed but that also meant that I had no chance at having a real relationship with another family, one that I could actually fit in with.

My family is full of outgoing and fun-filled people. I am not like that at all. I do like to have fun and go out but I am also an extremely shy person. I love to read and write. I would rather be alone with my boyfriend most of the time than spend some time downstairs with my immediate family. I get extremely annoyed by them but that's okay I guess, since they say that I am a mean person who likes to speak to no one. That's not my fault, though. If they want to speak to me they shouldn't be so mean themselves. I love to go hang out with the rest of my family, though, like my tios, tias and cousins.

When I was younger, I used to get picked on in school and at home by my sisters. I look like my dad and he is a hairy person. So since I came out like him I am kinda hairy too. I used to have a unibrow and I have hairy arms. In elementary school, some of the kids used to make fun of me because of my arms. They called me a monkey or a gorilla and it really hurt my feelings. At home my sisters used to make fun of my unibrow. They told me that I only had one eyebrow and that I was ugly and I always used to go to my parents crying about it. My dad always made me feel better, though. He told me that I was the prettiest out of all his daughters because I had my unibrow and I reminded him of himself. I always felt better after talking to him. Even though my dad did comfort me, my sisters still made fun of me. I never did tell anyone that I got made fun of because of my arms. I guess I found it too embarrassing to tell anyone in my family and I didn't want to give my two sisters any new ideas. As a result of being made fun of, as I got older I started shaving my arms and waxing my unibrow. I got tired of being called hairy so I decided to just take it all off. As I grew even older, I realized that I shouldn't care about how my arms look. I eventually stopped shaving but I still do wax my unibrow so no one where I live now even knows that I used to have one. My boyfriend never even knew I had a unibrow until a few days ago when I told him, and I've known him for three years now.

My immediate family thinks that I am an antisocial person. I don't really think I am. I do admit that I am shy, but I will speak to a person when I feel like it or if I really have to. They only think that because that is how they see me. In school I am a different person. Especially when I am not around my sisters. I talk to people and have conversations with them. Just because I don't feel like doing that at times doesn't mean that I am antisocial. They were actually pretty surprised when I got pregnant. Well, my parents were at least. When I got pregnant I was scared to tell anyone. All I could think about was what I was going to do. I had gone to a place called Planned Parenthood and I expected for everything be perfectly fine. I didn't think the test would come out positive. I had gone with a friend who is like a sister to me. Her name is Stephanie Rodriguez. She lived with my family at the time. She had been to Planned Parenthood before so I thought it would be easier to bring her along. I felt so out of place being there. I felt so young and as if I were being watched and judged by every person in there. When they called me to take the test, I didn't really think much about it. But waiting for the results felt like the years were passing by. Then the nurse there finally came out with my results. She told me that the test had come out positive and that I was two months pregnant. I am currently eight months (34 weeks) pregnant. I swear that after I heard those words come out of her mouth, I shut everything else out. I was paralyzed with fear and didn't know what to do. I walked out of that office and lied to the girl who was like my sister. I told her the test had come out negative. I didn't know what else to do. I had to tell my boyfriend first and I think anticipating how he was going to react took a few years off of my life.

I told him the next time I saw him and we just sat there for a bit. I didn't know how he was going to react. He decided that he had to tell his mom. The next time I saw her, I had never been so scared of seeing a person in my life. I didn't know how she was going to react to the news that her son had gotten his girlfriend pregnant. I didn't think she would even want to speak to me about it. When I saw her, she had waited until I got into the car and we drove off before even mentioning my pregnancy. It took so long for her to say anything that I was beginning to wonder if he had even told her. But he did tell her and after I knew that she knew, it didn't seem so bad anymore. She decided that we had to tell my parents. I remember wanting to cry at the idea of even facing them with this news. I couldn't tell them myself. I was too ashamed of what they would say and couldn't bare the faces I knew I would get from them. I couldn't tell them myself, so I had my boyfriend and his mom do it. While I waited in that car, all I could do was try to keep the tears from spilling out of my eyes. When my boyfriend and his mom came back to the car, they told me that my parents had started crying and all I wanted to do then was cry too. They took me home and I decided to tell everyone there the news. I didn't see the point in keeping it from them any longer. My boyfriend and his mom had left and then they came back with food they had gotten me. When they returned, it was his mom who got out of the car and brought me the food. She told me she knew that I was scared and that was the first time that I had hugged her and cried to her. She told me everything would be all right.

When my parents came home that night, they took me upstairs to their room and asked me a whole bunch of questions, none of which I had a good answer to.

We all cried and then after we finished crying we just accepted it. We had to face that there was nothing else we could do about it. That night was the first of the next few nights that I cried myself to sleep. I wasn't crying because I was upset about being pregnant. I cried because I had made my parents cry and that's the last thing I ever hoped to do. My boyfriend Marquell also had a hard time accepting it. At the time, he thought he had ruined my life because I was so young and having a child. I always told him that he didn't ruin anything. That I could still be everything I dreamed of being, only I would just have to work a lot harder at achieving it. Aubrey, that's what we are going to name her, is just going to push me to work harder. I don't think he thinks that he ruined my life anymore. Well, at least I hope he doesn't. He just made it 10 times better. I know this little girl of ours is going to be one of the best things that has ever happened to me. I wouldn't have the chance to have her with out my wonderfully amazing boyfriend, so I have him to thank.

Marquell thinks that I am antisocial too. He thinks he knows everything about me, just like my family. It's actually extremely annoying because I feel like they barely know me at all at times. He is the father of my child to be. I have known him since I was 12 years old. He just turned 18 a few days ago. We went out two times before but they didn't really work. He is a little hard to stand at times but I would rather have him in my life than have him out of it. My mom is OK with him and I don't really think that my dad likes him. I don't care. Though. They can't tell me who I can and can't see. It's not them dating the person. I'm not really that close to his family but I guess I'm to blame for that. Before I mentioned that I was extremely shy, so that means I don't get comfortable around new people too fast. Even though I have known them for about three years now, I still barely speak to them as if I've known them for that long. I think it's because it's my boyfriend's family and I just don't want them to think I'm some crazy, weird girl. It's not that I don't want to get comfortable around them, it's just that it's hard for me to get comfortable around anyone who isn't related to me. That's why I love Marquell so much. He is the one person who I am not related to that I am completely myself around. He does know me pretty well, but that doesn't mean he knows me completely.

I have one serious problem with him, though. He has really bad anger issues. That is the one thing that I hate about him. He gets mad so fast and sometimes it is completely unnecessary. That is why our relationship didn't work out the first two times. He says he had changed but we both know he hasn't. The only reason I am going out with him again is because I know he is at least trying to work on it. But I'm not one of those stupid girls who stays with a guy who hits them because they love him. If Marquell ever touches me or tries to, I will report him to the police in a heartbeat. I don't care that he is the father of my child. If he thinks he can put his hands on me, what is going to stop me from thinking that he won't put his hands on my daughter? I love him and everything, but I have no problem sending him to jail. Even though he has his anger issues, I don't think that he will ever hit me. He is the sweetest, most lovable person when he wants to be. He would do absolutely anything for me and that is one of the reasons I fell so in love with him. Yeah I might be young, but that doesn't mean that I can't be in love or know what it feels like. Also, just because I do love him doesn't mean we are going to be together forever. I never know what is going to happen in the future, but for now I'm happy with him and that's all that really matters. I wouldn't want it any other way.

This is my life. These people and experiences make me who I am. I have them to thank for the person I am today. Without them, who knows where or what I would be doing. My life so far may not have gone how I expected it to go, but I honestly couldn't care less. Whatever happens, happens. This is just my life now. Who knows what the future holds. But as I said before, whatever happens,

 happens. I know that no matter what, though, I'll be okay. I'll always try to make the best out of a bad situation.

I am Jessica Gomez

soundcloud.com/a-picture-is-worth/jessica

Long Live Edgardo

Hello there, my name is Edgardo Josue Herrera Murga. I like my name (lol); I kinda like my name. I shortened it for sure though. Can you imagine me trying to hit on a girl and she asks for my name and I'm like Edgardo Josue Herrera Murga? That wouldn't work out well. So, you can call me Edgardo Herrera. Do not call me Josue or we might just have to throw it down. I don't really have a significant attachment to it; I was born with it. I would not change it for the world though. I'm Edgardo, that's who I am and who I'll be.

I was born on July 3rd, 1995, in Hartford, Connecticut, so that makes me 17 years of age. Ever since then my mother has been with the biggest pain in her butt. She loves me though; well, I hope she does. She honestly has been a role model to me because it amazes me how someone can go through so much horror and not become it. She survived through the storm, fell a couple times but she arose as a queen and I was her little prince trying to defend her because the man I'm supposed to call my father was too big of a bitch to be a man to us. But we'll talk about that later on.

One gift or curse that I've been blessed or cursed with is speaking. I can talk for days! I feel like that is one of my strongest qualities. I'm a people person who enjoys interacting with others. That's just who I am. I'm constantly being told that I'll make a great politician because of the way I talk and persuade people to follow what I do. So who knows? One day you might just see me on TV representing my people.

There is a lot about me that no one knows, like a complete side that's overcast by the loud and obnoxious teenager everyone knows. Unfortunately you'll get to know some more of me.

Family. Well, my family is all over the place. I only consider the people who have been with me through the thick and thin. Honestly my godparents and godbrothers and sister have been more family than my grandparents and aunts. They're always there to knock some sense into me. I love them though. I know all they want from me is to be successful and they expect nothing less. Sometimes I feel like the expectations are too high but I'm gonna do whatever it takes to meet their expectations.

Parents. My parents, man I feel bad for them. I am the biggest pain in their butt. They love me though. We've been through hell and back. I can honestly say that my parents are my best friends. I can vent out to them about everything and anything. My dad is not my biological father, but I always say, "A father is not the one who makes but the one who raises." So yeah, I love him; he has always been there. He taught me how to shave my pencil mustache, gave me tips on how to pick up a couple of chicks. He's teaching me how to drive. He is my father. I can write a whole book about my mother; she's been my mother, best friend and father for a little while. She is strong and independent. She always pushes me to do better and expects nothing less than greatness from me. Sometimes it feels as if I can never satisfy them or I'll never meet their expectations because they expect so much from me. It gets very overwhelming at times and sometimes I rebel so they know I'm me and not the perfect child they'd hope

I become. We are always bumping heads because of that. Because I was taught and raised different, but yet I still manage to go against everything they have taught me. It drives my father insane, but I have a different way of seeing things, I guess.

I feel like in society it is not OK for young people to think differently or to speak our minds, and that is one of the main reasons why everyone rebels. Because they refuse to let anyone steal their right. The same rights soldiers are dying for, giving their lives to defend these rights and I feel that it is my duty as an American citizen to exercise that right. So for that reason I will speak my mind and I will speak up when I feel that something is wrong.

Community. My community, man there is so much to say about Reading, Pennsylvania. Reading is constantly being portrayed as this dangerous city with no hope. Well I strongly disagree. I would look you in the eyes and tell you that you don't know anything about my city because unlike a lot of people I take pride in where I'm from and I truly believe that if Reading has one thing, it is hope. There is talent everywhere. We have beautiful singers, gifted painters, dedicated athletes and really good writers. We have hardworking fathers doing whatever it takes to support their family, teaching their sons how to be men, gentlemen and fathers teaching them to work hard, and that if they walk and carry themselves well, then God's goodness will come to them. Mothers passing down their morals to daughters so that they respect themselves and walk in this world like a princess. So don't you ever tell me that the city of Reading does not have hope, 'cause that is a waste of time, or that there is no point in moving business to the city because the reason why there is so much hustling going on is because fathers will do whatever it takes

 to support their family. Bring more jobs in and I promise you that the crime rate will decrease rapidly and radically.

I am Edgardo Herrera

soundcloud.com/a-picture-is-worth/edgardo

My Life

My name is José Israel Jaime. I'm a Dominican, tall and the so-called class
clown. Many people call me Elmo. I don't
mind the nickname; it's actually very
funny to me. The name Elmo was given
to me by a girl in middle school when
she saw me without glasses, and since
everyone says I look like Elmo I decided
to keep the name. I've had the name for
about six years now and I really got
hooked to it. People call me Elmo more
than they call me José, but if I had a
chance I would change my name to my
middle name. My first name is too common so it bothers me going out and
hearing "José" and I'm standing in the
middle looking stupid.

There are so many things I've done in
my lifetime but the hardest thing I ever
had to do was probably leave my mother
and New York to move to Reading with
my grandmother. I mean in a way I am
sad that I left but if I really think about
it, moving here kept me out of trouble,
helped me meet new people, helped me
in school and helped me find out what I
wanted to do in college. So in a way
moving to Reading was one of the best
things that happened to me. I'm a person who hates being bored, and I can't
stay still, so I tend to walk around and

distract other students for me and their entertainment. So I would have to say that my strongest quality is entertainment. It's good though, because my dream is to be a professional wrestler and that is one of the most important things to do (entertain).

There are some days that I get very lazy but what motivates me to do my work is knowing that the more I work, the closer I get to college, which means I'm getting closer to wrestling school. I'm the type of person who would rather listen to rock music more than anything else. I don't have a favorite song but I do have a favorite band and it is Linkin Park. One of the perks of being a pro wrestler is that I would get to travel the world, because the farthest I've been was to the Dominican Republic and I want to see more of the world.

I always get asked where do I see myself in 5 to 10 years and I always say holding the heavyweight championship above my left shoulder. It feels like no one believes me so I want to prove the nonbelievers wrong, and this is also what motivates me to become a pro wrestler.

I love many things but if I had to choose one I would choose family. I have one brother and two sisters. There are many words to describe my family but if I had to chose one it would be "awesome." They are always there when I need them, even if the situation is horrible they are they supporting me through the ups and downs. I remember when I used to live in New York, and my brother got fired from his job at Gamestop. My mother told him everything is going to be OK and bought him a phone plus found him another job. (She's so awesome.) My mother is my hero. She took care of her four children without any help from my father and we all came out well educated and well mannered. I'm so proud of her. She is the reason why I want to become something big in life, for I can repay her for everything she has done for my siblings and me. She will always come first in my life, and I'm doing whatever I can to make her happy.

My community is actually very decent. I first lived behind the Glenside Elementary School. It was quiet and boring so all I did was ride my bike but then my grandmother got a call saying that they had a house for her in Glenside. From the stories I heard as a kid I was nervous to even step in the hood/projects. I thought I was going to get hurt my first week so I didn't come out for about a month, but this neighborhood is actually very chill. I mean it could have been better but people started to move out and the newbies never want to come so it's always boring. I would give more programs to Glenside, for when it's boring people could entertain. The park is divided into two parts: The little kids are all at the playground and the teens are always by the courts, but it's always safe for the kids to play.

The holiday that is most celebrated in my neighborhood is the 4th of July. Everyone gets together and celebrates. Everyone is usually inside on Christmas but everyone is drinking and dancing on New Year's Eve. I like my community and am always outside playing basketball, football or baseball. We love playing sports. It entertains us, but basketball is our main sport.

One of the things that surprises me the most is that people and programs love to come to Glenside to give us food or just to give out drinks. The things I don't like

are that the little kids are being influ-
enced with bad things constantly, and
kids look at you telling you to move out
the way and if you don't they start cursing at you for no reason. But other than
that the community is really good. I got
used to it. If I could fix Reading I would
try to take out the bad influences.

 Now you know a huge part
of my life and everything
going on in it.

I am José Jaime

soundcloud.com/a-picture-is-worth/jos-jaime

How I Became Awesome

My family is close, a little too close. It's a little uncomfortable to know that your mom knows what you are always doing. My dad on the other hand is not my father. It's a shame for me to say that. My father comes later but I will tell you how my dad is not my father.

It happened when I was 6. I hardly remember, but I do remember my mom yelling at my dad, then she left and my dad told my brother and me to go to the car. He drove us to a house and I remember my dad introduced me to a lady. He told my brother and me that she was our new mom. I had no feelings toward this because I was little. I disliked my mom a little because she was doing her job as a mom. I could tell that my brother was confused and angry. My mom soon came to the house of my "new mom." My mom came into the house very angry and began to hit my dad with a lamp. I forgot what happened to my "new mom." My mom had it with my dad because this was the third time he had cheated on her.

My mom moved my brother and me to an apartment. That day I cried for my dad, and my mom gave me her phone so that I could call him. After a few months, my brother and I were able to go to my dad's house, which was exactly how I left it. My dad looked the same but he was so happy to see us. I was depressed by everything: my brother, bullies, and my mom and dad separating. I was so tired of my life I would drag my body around. I had the most difficult stage of my life and just thinking of it I can feel the punches and the ridicule most days. I'm happy but when I'm alone I break down and cry, never letting others know of my situation because of my pride, I think. I know my mom did the right thing but I still feel my life would be different if she had stayed. Now I hate my dad but he is my dad so I can't turn my back on him. I will never go to his level.

At least my first neighbors were nice. I remember that I would hang out over my neighbors' houses having sleepovers, playing in the park, you name it we did everything until my mom and dad split. When my brother, mom and I moved to an apartment, we knew nobody except the drug addict on the first floor. The funny thing I didn't realize after we moved to the house was that two houses down, things had changed a lot in my dad's neighborhood. Everybody would look at us as if we did something to them. I couldn't wrap my mind around it, but then I couldn't stop them from thinking what they wanted to think. My old friends always looked at me with a dirty look. We never hung out again. It seemed like I was cut out from the world and it hurt in a weird way. After two to three years of living in that apartment, my brother, mom and I moved to a house. Moving there made me have a different outlook of my life, if you will.

I suck up the pain of the past and embrace it to be a better person. My future stepfather moved across the street. My brother and I never got along but my stepbrother and I are like two peas in a pod. He and I did everything: sports, video games, you name. We understand each other. When it came to my stepfather I quickly respected him. How or why I can't remember but he is a good father. They moved in and it was the best.

In school I was known as the cool kid with bad grades, but I don't care because it was not important to me at all. At home I could do whatever because my mom was going to school and work and my stepfather is always on the move, so I had no rules in my home.

My dad is a weird human. He loves me but he shows it the worst way possible. He's the worst dad. He should never have had children. Not that he abused me but that he neglects me and it would be better if I never met him. But then I hope I'm wrong. My brother is a clone of my dad; he does not care about anyone but himself and worst of all he makes bad decisions for himself, and that goes for both of them. This happened not too long ago: My brother stole his brand new laptop on eBay for less than what he could buy the iPad2. My dad bought a dirty broken boat that needs a ton of repairs but he got it cheap during the winter. When summer came along he put no effort into trying to fix it, then wondered why we did not go fishing that summer.

My mom is my rock. She is my dad and my mom. Without her I do not know where I would be. Even when my stepfather was in the picture, she acted like my dad and mom for a while. I never saw my mom cry. When I think of my mom, I think of someone so strong. When we moved out of my dad's house, my look showed that I was happy she got rid of him. I thought that my mom would never get a guy but thankfully she did.

My stepfather is my dad. He is my father and male role model. I'm thankful that he came 'cause that time was the part of my life when I didn't know where I stood. I was rebellious and my mom did not have time with school and work, but he had the time of day and he cared.

I am Kevin Jendrus

soundcloud.com/a-picture-is-worth/kevin

Coming to America

My name is Davell Lawrence. I am 18 years of age and was born on June 30, 1994, in Kingston, Jamaica, and lived there since I was 10 years old before immigrating to the United States. Both of my parents were born in Jamaica and I lived with my dad before coming to the U.S. to live with my mom. I have two sisters and two brothers, and am the oldest out of all of them.

Living in Jamaica, times were tough. We weren't poor but it was a struggle and sometimes we had to hustle to make ends meet. Even though it was just my dad and me, we still had other family members who we had to help out because our family is a close one that always sticks together.

Now that I'm in the U.S., it's my job to take this opportunity and become someone in life so I can help my family to get out of the struggle. When I was living in Jamaica times were much rougher than here in the U.S. Sometimes it would be hard for my dad to find sufficient work from his job because he is a motor vehicle insurance agent. Even though times were rough, we always made ends meet and I was able to go to a good private school. I was always able to get a good education, a bright student finishing in the top five in all grades from first to sixth. Knowing that the times I faced were rough, school was my family and my exit ticket. I was living in good conditions and going to good schools, while knowing that there were better conditions and more opportunities.

My family is everything to me; they mean the world to me. I am the oldest of my siblings, and have two brothers and two sisters, three living with me and one in England. I live with three of my siblings who are from my mother's side; my sister who lives in England is from my dad's side and she lives with her mom. As the oldest sibling I hope to be a positive role model in their lives, and encourage them to do well, become successful and achieve their life goals. I care a lot for my family, especially for my siblings because they are the younger ones. My father is the most important and influential person in my life. He has been there since day one and is still there for me now. I've been everywhere with my father, living with him since the day I was born until I was 10 and moved to the U.S.

Coming to America was very difficult for me to adapt. The culture is very different than in Jamaica. When I started school at Riverside Elementary in the 5th grade, I was very different from the other students. I spoke a different way and it was very hard for people to understand some of the things I said. It was a little difficult to make friends because I was different. For me I think school in America was easier for me than in Jamaica. Academics were a lot harder there and I still managed to maintain good grades. When I moved here, I realized that my behavior started to change and it wasn't pleasant. With me trying to make friends, I tried to be cool with everyone else and would do things that I knew were wrong. I would act up in school, steal, fight and other behavioral issues. These problems that I set on myself have caused me to be kicked out of school twice, been put on probation, kicked out of my house, locked up in jail and sent back to Jamaica. Through all that I went through for my wrongdoings, it took me a while to figure out that what I was doing was not right and that I'm only hurting myself. I realized doing all those things doesn't make me cool and being myself was all I needed to do to be my own cool and have positive friends around me to do good and steer me in the right direction. I learned to keep distractions away and focused on school and family.

I've always been in a good community here and in Jamaica, surrounded by good people and in a safe neighborhood. In Jamaica, my community was very caring;

everyone knew everybody and were all friends. We held many community events and gatherings such as picnics, Earth Day cleanups and fun days. I remember a time on Earth Day: Every person on our block came out and cleaned up our environment. My dad cooked food for everyone and we all had a good time and acted together as a family.

I like to partake in various activities. My hobbies include basketball, soccer, volunteering and church activities. I like helping others and my church. Helpful things that I've done include helping out at a restaurant, helping with a food bank and coaching my little brother's elementary school basketball team. I enjoy working with little kids and helping people who are less fortunate, by making a difference and being a positive influence in their lives. Making other people happy is what makes me happy. Doing so makes me feel good about myself that I'm doing good things instead of doing something negative.

My goals in life are my main focus and I am determined to achieve them. I hope after graduation to attend college and study in the field of criminal justice. My career choice is hopefully to become a private investigator and work for the FBI or CIA. I hope to attend Villanova University after I spend two years in community college. I hope to achieve all my goals and become successful in life, to become a positive figure in others' lives and set standards for how things should be done. I am a good person who has made mistakes in life and is steering my path in the right direction to be a better man.

I am Davell Lawrence

My Real-Life Story

In Haiti where I grew up, life wasn't offering me a feeling to keep fighting for what I want or what I wanna be. The biggest thing I couldn't stand in my country but had to deal with was its students who had great skills, students who want to learn the best they could, but they didn't have the opportunity.

The reason I started to explain about education is because when I was in my country's school, it wasn't like I observed it right now in Pennsylvania. I remember that I used to walk like 20.25 miles. I used to get up around 4 in the morning to start walking, and after school on the way home I saw other students who used to be my friends with their parents who came to pick them up. I do not feel like my parents should also have picked me up, but that made me feel something deeply in my heart, like even my parents didn't come. I didn't give up. I was still keeping up, all that experience gave me the opportunity to understand better that I have to work hard and be smart to be what I wanna be. I think also that my country's government doesn't really have a base. They don't really think about the beauty that a country could have; they just come to get their pockets full and disappear. When they run for the first time they come with every word and make people believe in them. They know how to pretend to make people believe that they could change everything, after they won the election. A few days later they forgot those words that they pretended to tell with their heart. I think that in my country we still had an unproductive and unsuccessful government, but that didn't make me feel like giving up. I keep it up and God blesses my family. God opens the door for us. My parents brought me to the United States for a better education.

On the other hand, my life in Haiti was hell on earth. I remember a day when I lived alone without anyone to support me, but I started to understand why the reason that I was living by myself is that my father had eight children. I'm his fifth son. My father wasn't really worried about me, but I won't regret that I'm still loving him. Maybe he doesn't know yet how to talk about it. I hope that one day he has awareness to come to me and talk about it.

I remember when I was 5 years old my father left. He just left my mom and me in the house as a little boy. I didn't really know what it means to live without a father, but I miss him a lot. When I saw other friends with their parents, at those moments I felt sad because my mom was everything; she played the father role, but I didn't really know how my mom felt at the time. I could feel she needed something, some help, but I couldn't do anything.

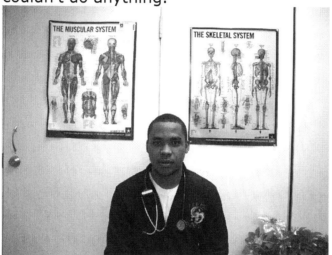

Now I really understand that in life you've got to be a man, but to be a man you have to fight for it. I've decided to reach my goals and am prepared to face any obstacle in life. My mother always told me as a boy to count my blessings. And I always saw my mother try to keep her principles. She always made sure that I went to school every day, that I did my homework and studied, that I ate normally every day. All that stuck in my brain. I don't wanna see myself get low. I like my educational success, and all the advice that she showed me. I have to make that work in practice. I'm not saying that I have to be like her, but to be a better person.

I remember a day when I saw my father. I was 7 years old. (He left when I was only 4.) He saw me after 3 years, and slid his hand on top of my head, then told me, "Hey, my boy's grown a lot. I'm glad to see you." He talked to my mother a few minutes then left. I watched him go and I think when I talked to him I smelled something. I had no idea, but it sure wasn't perfume. Now I know it was alcohol.

I don't let all that get to me. I just choose to make my mother proud of me and make her happy, now that I'm in the United States.

I am Jean Mouscardy

soundcloud.com/a-picture-is-worth/jean

"There is no greater agony than bearing an untold story inside you."
                                    —*Maya Angelou*

My Own History

My name is Jheyler Alcantara Perez. I was born in Miches Seibo/Dominican Republic, on November 18, 1995. I am an Adventist of Seven Days and grew up in Seibo/Miches, a small town of Santo Domingo, where I would always go to the river with my family and friends because it is so close to my house.

My family consists of five people: my parents Hector E. Alcantara and Luz Nereida Perez; two brothers, Edwin G. Alcantara, 19 years old, and Emmanuel Alcantara, 14. We all grew up in Miches and they are Adventists of Seven Days like me. My father and mother are the best parents in the world because they are so protective of our family and they want us to be well always.

We have only separated once in our lives, when my parents came to Pennsylvania and we stayed in Puerto Rico with my grandmother for eight months. We missed our parents a lot, then we came and were reunited again and I felt very happy because I was back with my parents.

They are my life. Without them I do not know what I would do because they are the biggest supporters that I have in my life. They always tell me to fight for what I want and never give up, because to be a success in life I have to work hard and always keep trying.

I remember going to many Camp Conquerors, where I had good times growing up. I remember as if it were today. In camp we went to the river to fetch water and slippery vajada, which was fine but when we came with water and one slipped, we would all fall into the river. I was laughing but at the same time I was mad because I had fallen.

When I was 13, I went with my family to the Conquerors National Camp in the Dominican Republic. That was so good for my family and me because we had a good experience and many memories of that camp. My best friend from my childhood was Jose G. de la Cruz, my neighbor. He and I did a lot of mischief in the neighborhood like throwing stones on the roofs of the neighbors at night, because they bothered us by telling my parents that we threw some nonsense into their backyard.

When little, I was a very problematic child who wanted to fight. I had many fights; my first fight was at 8 years old with a boy, the second at 10 with a girl. I wanted to separate a fight and she hit me. Well, my brother and I fought two guys who did not want to but we went to their neighborhood because they were the leaders of that block and had said that if we go through their neighborhood that they would get us "a trompadas," which means cuffs. The next day we returned there, not because we wanted to fight but because my brother had a girlfriend in that block and then we realized that one of the boys was in love with my brother's girlfriend and that's why we had to fight with them. We did not feel that we should fight if they wanted to fight and we defended ourselves.

The next fight was with a boy. I fought him because he was looking for trouble with my brothers and I gave him what he deserved. Two years later he was killed from 16 stab wounds because he sold drugs and made enemies.

When I was in eighth grade, I had the most dangerous fight. I remember that I broke his head with a rock and he hit me with a stick on my arm; I was so mad at him. I fought with him because he began to annoy my girlfriend, but then I realized that she cheated on me with that boy and from that moment on I realized that you should not fight without knowing all the facts.

I had many experiences with brides, as fights and problems, so I decided to be alone for a while till I finished my studies in high school. I also realized that brides can be a distraction in school.

When I lived in the Dominican Republic, I was more comfortable there than here in the U.S. because I did not have to speak a language that I did not know. I could express or talk with anyone with confidence because I knew they would not laugh at me. When I came to the U.S., I had to learn to express myself in English classes. It is so difficult for me because I can't speak English like I can speak Spanish, but I am improving.

I moved to Puerto Rico on October 14, 2010. There are many differences in these two countries. Puerto Rico's currency is the dollar and Dominican Republic's is the Dominican peso. Also, as far as speaking English and Spanish, Dominicans only speak Spanish. There are many qualities between the two countries, such as that they speak Spanish, are Latin countries and are neighbors.

My community here has more children in the streets, and more people smoking weed. The community there in Puerto Rico is like in the Dominican Republic, because everybody helps each other and has some respect, but I like more the community of D.R. because we felt more safe because and not as many people are killed like in P.R. I liked when I was in D.R. I went to the beach and rivers anytime, because they were so close to my house and I liked when I ascended the mango trees in the field.

I decided to come to the I-LEAD Charter School to find new opportunities for my education, because I want to learn in a school that is calm and without fights. I want to graduate high school and get my diploma, then I want to go to a good college like Penn State and graduate as an automotive engineer. Also, I want to be a professional basketball player in the NBA.

My dreams are to have my own house, get married, have my family and get my dream car, an Audi R8. I have a good girlfriend who is my best friend. I love her—Iveliz Melendez. She is Cuban and

Puerto Rican and so beautiful. She studies at the I-LEAD Charter School in 10th grade. We are members of the soccer team there.

I am Jheyler Alacantara Perez

soundcloud.com/a-picture-is-worth/jheyler

"Human beings are not born once and for all on the day their mothers give birth to them, but life obliges them over and over again to give birth to themselves."
—*Gabriel García Márquez*

A Picture Is Worth... 1,000 Words of Betania

I could never understand how I can love and hate something so much at the same time. My family: amazing, crazy, funny, weird, unusual, out of the ordinary and mine. Though my family isn't normal, I would not exchange them for anything in the world.

I have never seen my parents together, so I guess I never really had a chance to feel about their not being together. I am my mother's first, and my father's last... at least I think so. I was a "surprise" as mother likes to put it. She was 18 when she had me and my father was 34. Big age difference, 16 years to be exact. My parents had broken up before they knew I existed, so it was difficult for them to understand, from what I know. Though I'm not positive, I'm pretty sure that I'm the result of an affair.

Both my parents are from the Dominican Republic, from San Pedro de Macoris. I was born July 31st in the Bronx, New York. I have many siblings; when I explain to people how many brother and sisters, I always separate them from my father's side and my mother's side. From my father's side, I have two beautiful older sisters named Perla, 20, and Ambar, 18. From my mother's side I have three beautiful younger siblings, Alexa, 11, Alexander, 4, and Allen, 3. As you can see, I'm the only one with an unusual name, Betania.

From what I understand, I was named by my great grandfather; Bethany in the Spanish form. My name is a city in Israel and you can find it in many places in the Bible. My mother was originally supposed to be named Genesis or Kayla. I really like those names and I wish she had stuck to it, because I used to get bullied because of it. I still kind of do to this day; I get called things like Petunia, Lasagna and Ventana ("window" in Spanish), which is why I have always wanted to change my name. Being bullied is not fun, obviously. I never really let anyone know that I felt some type of way about them calling me names, because I never wanted to seem weak to them or that they affect me.

I don't really communicate well with my older sisters or father. I think the main reason is because they live in Brooklyn, New York, and I live here. Before we moved to Pennsylvania, I hadn't seen my father for two years and two more when while I lived here. I met my sisters twice and I knew their names, so in 2011 I looked up my oldest sister's name, Perla, on Facebook and found her. I got so excited, I cried. I added her and she gave me my other sister Ambar's Facebook and we talked. I got my father's number and we arranged a meeting, and my mother made one too, but with the court. My mother made my father give child support, and I feel as if that's the only reason he came down to Reading, but then I have to think that my father is a better man than that. Now I only see them on some occasions like holidays and the summer. I miss them dearly and can't wait for school to be done and over with so I can go to New York. I don't think that's going to happen anymore due to court issues.

My family and I are somewhat close, but I'm closest to my younger siblings, since I don't really see my older sisters. When I do get the chance to be with them, we are close but I feel as if we are friends more than sisters since they have been together all their lives and I have only really known them for about two and a half years. In the future I hope to have a better relationship with all of my family, especially with my father and older sisters. I just want to have a normal broken-up family and be able to communicate frequently without any sign of awkwardness. It doesn't help that I'm awkward.

I don't really like my community. To me it is just ugly and not a very good environment to raise children, but it's what we have to deal with for now. We have many, many, many crackheads on my street but Reading, Pennsylvania, has proved itself to be beautiful on many occasions. Just a couple of days ago a professor from New York came and she taught photography and how to tell stories through pictures. Well, she and one of her students came over to my school and got the school to provide us with cameras and she took my classmates and I out to our community to capture pictures. I loved the program and you really get to see that anything can be picture-perfect and everything is beautiful in their own little way. It made me see my community differently and I appreciate her for that. I didn't like my pictures; at the moment that I captured the photos I thought they were amazing but then when I saw everyone else's, I lost all hope in my pictures. But now I know that Reading is equally messed up and beautiful.

Before moving to Reading, I lived in New York and it is really different compared to Pennsylvania. New York is always busy and there is always something to do and in Reading all there is to do is go to the mall, pool or the movies. At some point in my life, I would like to return to where I came from because I'm a bit confused as to where I'm from. I would like to say that I'm a girl from New York and I know all the streets and have that crazy New York accent and attitude, but I don't. Every time I head over there I am at a complete loss and don't know a damn thing, and I wish to change that. Before I die, I will learn the streets of New York.

I don't really know how to start off talking about myself. My name's Betania but you already know that. I'm Dominican. Already know that. Something you don't know is that I am a Christian. I'm a Seventh Day Adventist, to be exact. This plays a big role in my life because I'm not like the usual teenager. On Friday nights while all my school friends are out at the movies, parties, carnival, etc., I am usually at church. I got baptized last summer and my life has changed since then. In my religion the holy day is Saturday and we spend the whole day praising the Lord. When I say Saturday, I don't mean like at 12 a.m., I mean when the sun sets on Friday nights. That's why while people are out being teens, I'm at church. Don't get me wrong; I love going to church and I love everyone there, but sometimes I just want to go to the movies with everyone else.

I believe that because I don't go out with anyone from school, I don't have as many friends as before and that really hurts. I feel as if friends have abandoned me just because I don't go to the movies every weekend. I mean, I'm sorry, but that's my way of life and I am not thinking about changing it.

I would like to say that at the moment I am at the awkward stages of being a teenage girl. Some days I'm happy and some days I'm extremely sad and depressed, and sometimes both at the same time. I don't know if that's normal but I am pretty sure those weird feelings will pass by as I grow up. I'm pretty goofy. I love boy bands and random things like that, and the Internet has to be one of the best inventions ever. It has caused me much happiness and provides me with things that the outside can't. I also love reading; it is like I enter a stranger's world and I learn and feel their feelings. That is truly amazing. Call me ridiculous, but I'd rather read than go outside sometimes, and because of books I believe in true love.

I have my whole life planned out. I know exactly what I want to do and how I'm going to do it. I don't care what anyone else has to say; I will achieve these things. I plan on graduating early as a 16-year-old graduate. I just think it would be awesome to be the youngest person on campus and be able to do the same things as people who are years older than me. I look forward to setting an example to my younger siblings and prove to my mother that her children can make it and we will be successful, then return to her all that she has done for us. We may not fully understand everything that she has done for us, but we will someday return the favor.

In only my childhood, I have seen things that normal little girls aren't supposed to see and you wouldn't be able to tell by just looking at my face. I always try to keep a happy facial expression to keep people in the mindset that I am fine, but sometimes that comes and bites me in the butt. Like when I am really sad and at the point of going insane in my own head and I need someone to talk to, no one notices right off the bat. I always have to approach someone or they have to notice that I'm crying, because they automatically assume that I'm fine. I have no one else to blame but myself. I can honestly say that I have trouble expressing myself, and when I do it never ends well. That is why I want to become a psychologist, specifically for teens who have been through abuse, whether it's physical, emotional, verbal, etc., because I can relate and I know how it feels not to have anyone to approach when you have a problem. Hopefully I can make a difference in a young person's life in the future and maybe even save a life.

The thing I fear most is being easily replaced or forgotten. I want everyone who comes into my life to mean something and the same way for them. I don't know exactly what my future holds but I am hoping for all my goals to be accomplished, and every time I fall I will get  right back up again and keep going on.

This is my story and it has only just begun.

I am Betania Robles

soundcloud.com/a-picture-is-worth/betania

"For apart from inquiry, apart from the praxis, individuals cannot be truly human. Knowledge emerges only through invention and re-invention, through the restless, impatient, continuing, hopeful inquiry human beings pursue in the world, with the world, and with each other."

—Paulo Freire

The Path That I Walk On

Hi, my name is Pedro Antonio Sanchez. I'm 16 years old, and Dominican from my dad's side and Puerto Rican from my mom's. My parents are typical Spanish parents in that when they did hit me they would hit me with a chancleta (slipper). When I ate I would eat chuleta (pork chops with plantains). I like being in an all-Spanish family and having two languages that I am able to speak. I was born in Newark, NJ, on October 22, 1996 in Columbus Hospital. I have six brothers and sisters. I would have more but my mom lost one and she got three abortions from her stepdad; if they were alive I would have 10 brothers and sisters.

My mom had it rough coming from an all-Puerto Rican family. I don't like talking about my mom and her past because it's really rough and it hurts a lot to hear her say this stuff. It was hard for her but my dad had it rough too, coming from an all-Dominican family. Dominicans are tough and so strict with a lot of stuff and my dad's dad died before he was even born. My dad was born in "la capital" and had a kind of good life because he was rich at some point until his family found out that his father passed away. They then took the land, the money, everything that my grandfather had left my dad. But I'm glad that we're not rich because I don't want to be like all the rich people; for example, they are so greedy and cocky and always thinking about themselves. They think the world revolves around them. And that's why I am glad I am not rich nor poor but right where God wants us to be in the middle.

I'm used to being around everybody who I have been around. I like being half Puerto Rican and half Dominican. I like putting the two cultures together. I don't identify myself with only one race but prefer both. I love the different foods; I love my mom's cooking but don't see the difference, except the different holidays. Puerto Ricans celebrate "Dia de los Reyes" ("The Three Kings") and I know that all those holidays are very tradition-al to my family. But I don't celebrate those holidays because they are false like the three kings were in the Bible. It doesn't say that the men who went to see Jesus were kings, but rather wise men came to see him. And it doesn't even say three; it doesn't say any num-ber. The Bible just calls them wise.

Other than that what I want to talk about is my life and how I was and how I am now. So you know my name is Pedro and you know my background, but do you know the real me? It starts like this: I am a regular person like you who knows maybe we're facing the same problem. Who knows? Only the Lord knows and I don't mean to sound religious but God is real even though you don't believe he is still there. God is not going to stop being God just because one person doesn't believe in him.

For example, just because you don't see the air you're not going to believe that it's not there, but that's a whole different subject. Back to what I was saying, I may not have had a really rough childhood but I do have my struggles. I was born in Newark, NJ, with mom's name Beatrice, dad's name Pedro and my brother Chino and two sisters Diana and Rachel, but I have two more brothers and one more sister. I had a rough childhood. I was always picked on by people but you can say bullied.

I always tried to follow everybody else. I always wanted to fit in so badly. People would always pick on me, calling me shorty, toothpick, ugly, etc., etc. I knew I wasn't but those words got to me really badly so I did everything for those kids who always picked on me. I wanted them to not pick on me again so I started following the wrong people and started hanging out with the wrong crowd and doing the wrong things like smoking with my friends and drinking.

I wasn't the only one in the family who went through a rough childhood. My mom was raped at age 4 by her stepfather and by 16 she had three abortions from him. But also my dad Pedro suffered too. He didn't have a dad; his dad died before he was born so it was hard for him growing up without a father and having to take care of himself. He had to face many trials and started hustling in the streets in his mid- teens and getting into fights and gangs. And I know that many of you who are reading this book are probably struggling with the stuff that my family and I struggled with.

But there is a solution to all of these problems. Are you ready? Are you really ready? It's... Jesus. Wow, Jesus. I know you're probably thinking that what is this person talking about; he doesn't understand that everybody doesn't believe in God. Well I know that there are some of you who don't believe in God, but I can't keep my mouth shut for what he's done for me and my family. I know it's crazy to say, but God is real. If he can change me, he can change you.

There's no difference between you and me; we're both from the hood, both struggling with problems. Who knows? You're probably struggling with more problems than I struggled with, but there nothing impossible for God. You probably have an atheist mind but let me tell you something. I had an atheist mind as well. You see, I didn't always believe in God.

I went through a lot, like being bullied, getting into fights, being sick and having to deal with a lot of stuff. I mean, I tried a lot of stuff to ease out the pain, like trying to kill myself three times and even running away. But even if I tried I always failed. I didn't know what was it but I knew that all of my attempts were not successful and even to this day I don't understand why I'm still alive.

But I do know something: If it wasn't for the mercy of God I wouldn't be here. I know people may think, *Look at this religious person talking about God*. But can I say this: I'm not religious and I would never be. I just have a relationship with God. I am not Catholic, I am Pentecostal and I believe in the Word 100%.

I had a dream about the Lord. I was in my house hanging out. It felt like summer, about 82 degrees. It was pretty good out, so I remember my mom calling all of the family in the house to eat and while we prayed for the food, my eyes went to the corner and there I saw a shadow. While they were still praying, I went over to see who it was. I saw this guy standing there and as soon as I saw him I fell back and saw him reach out his hand to pick me up. And when he picked me up, I was in total shock. He then gave me a big hug and when I mean a big hug, he really did, because I've hugged a lot of people before but I can't compare his hug to anybody else's. It was as if love was hugging you. And after the hug he looked at me and said he loved me. When he said that I felt like something came alive in me. I don't know what it was but I felt it. Jesus walked to my dining room to come eat with us. As he's doing that, I'm here thinking to myself, *Is this real? Is this really happening to me? Am I in front of Jesus himself?*

Well to tell you the truth I was in front of Jesus and he is real because that was real. And when he got to the table, he already started talking to my family and he got along well with them. He made my father laugh and he said some stuff to make my mom cry tears of joy and he

made my sister feel so important. You
see, we all matter in the eyes of God.

We are all equal like the Bible says: nobody higher than nobody. Also notice
that the Bible says in John 3:16 that for
God so loved the world he gave his only
begotten son, that whoever would believe in him would have eternal life. But
notice how it says he loved the world,
not only one person, not only me and not
only you, but both of us. And when I saw
him eating and talking to my family as if
he was a part of my family, it really got
to me and made me think that of all
places, God chose me and my family to
come visit and tell me how much he
loves us. The Lord came and left, but I
know he's coming back for me so I'm
getting ready now, just like we all
should.

My path is a lot of tears and happiness,
and by me making this book I can tell
you that the Lord has been and he will
always be with me to the ends of the
earth.

Knowing your path, that you struggle, is
hard. Mine was hard too, and though I'm
still walking on mine and am not done, I
can say that this path leads to something. Do you really want to know what it
leads to? Start walking. Let God lead the
way like the Bible says: Jesus is the way,

the truth and the light. Nobody comes to the Father but through him.

I am Pedro Sanchez

soundcloud.com/a-picture-is-worth/pedro

"The only thing that I have done that is not mitigated by luck, diminished by good fortune, is that I persisted, and other people gave up."

—*Harrison Ford*

Life Is Precious

My name is Precious-Anastasia De'Lin Sewell. I love my first and middle names, but not my last. My name tells what my mom thought of me when she gave birth. My mom thought I was a precious baby. If possible, I would have chosen to have my mother's last name instead of my father's. I don't want people to know that I am related to him. I am my mother's child.

The hardest thing I have ever done is told my dad I no longer want to have contact with him. Doing it was only hard because he cried. I've never seen a man cry until that day. It was for the better but it still hurt. He was a negative toxin in my life that just needed to go. I felt great after I did it, like a huge weight was lifted from my shoulders.

My dream is to be my own person and to show everyone that it's possible to come up from nothing. I was born and raised in Reading, PA. I have one sibling on my mom's side, and 40+ from my dad's. I wish I only had my brother from my mom's side; that would have saved me a lot of hurt. All my dad's kids were taken from my life when he went to prison. Even before he went away, I knew it was going to happen eventually. I was hoping it was after I turned 18 so I could adopt them all, but that didn't happen. Every day I think about them, but there is nothing I can do to change the situation we're in.

My parents are no longer together; they broke up when I was 9. I am happy that my parents aren't together. My dad wasn't good enough for my mother. My dad was a serious piece of shit. My mom did everything for him, including raising his kids and he was just so unapprecia-tive. He physically and verbally abused her, but all she did was love him. I used to think that my mom was stupid for staying, but it's not her fault. She want-ed me to have my parents together and she was in love. Love is blind. My par-ents' relationship doesn't affect the way I see all relationships. I don't compare an-yone to them; they're unique.

When my parents split up, my dad told me I had two options. I could either live with him full-time or do one week on, one week off. All I wanted to do was live with my mom. The first time I ever went to my dad's new house, his girlfriend didn't even know who I was; she thought he didn't have any other children. If he wanted me there so bad, you'd think he would at least tell her about me. She was irrelevant to me anyways, because she wasn't my mother. Nothing that ever came out of her mouth was of any importance to me. I barely even remember that woman. It was just hurtful that my dad never brought me up to her, like I was nonexistent. I swear my dad only wanted me there because he knew it would make me unhappy. Or maybe it was to piss my mom off, I'll never know. My dad moved to the other side of town, so I had to move to another school, which was way different than what I was used to. It was closer to the ghetto side of town so people were a lot meaner. The streets over there were dirty and the kids acted inappropriately. It was much different from what I grew up around. Where I used to live in Reading, the sidewalks were clean, the children were well behaved, and you didn't hear about much violence. It seemed like the perfect place to live. This new place was a nightmare to me. I started to hear curse words from people who weren't yet adults and met people who didn't like me just because of the way I looked. It was the first time that I realized we really do live in a cruel world. My new community had some nice neighbors, though. I eventually made very good friends with them.

In my new school, 10th & Penn, a lot of people didn't like me. They said it was because I acted better than them. I really think it was because I was just well

behaved and didn't do any of the stupid
things they wanted me to do. My brother, sister and I were all in the same
grade in this school, so I never had to
worry about being alone. That was the
only good part. Other than that, I hated
just about everything. There I got in my
first physical fight trying to protect my
brother, Tiger, who was a little mentally
challenged. That's when I found my vio-
lent side. From there I pretty much
wanted to fight anyone for absolutely
anything. It was what I became known
for. I stayed that way until my second
year in high school. Now I know that no
one is worth getting in enough trouble
that I could ruin my future.

When I first started middle school, I
went to the Gateway School for the Per-
forming Arts. That school was one of the
best things that has ever happened to
me. It was my two favorite things in one

place, school and music. Singing was my passion for a while when I was younger, but I knew it wasn't practical to try and make a career out of it. For my second and third year of middle school, I went to Southern Middle School, the most fun time of my life. It was a whole bunch of people expressing their individuality. Everything was great until my last year there when we first began school. A lot of people knew that my dad had just gone to jail before school started and it was the talk of the town.

When my dad was shown on the news because of the negative things he had done, it was so embarrassing. How could someone who I was supposed to look up to do such a bad thing? Everyone thinks it's funny to joke about being a pimp until someone you know goes to jail for it. It is not a funny situation! People who were around my age when it happened were so immature, so they joked about it for a while. It just made me angry knowing that no matter what I do, I will always have a permanent connection with him.

Everyone was saying that I was going to be just like him. I learned to deal with that and just went on with my school year. Once the middle of the year came, some girl decided that she wanted to tell me how bad a person I was because he was my dad. I couldn't help the family I was born into. I was so upset after that; there was no way I wanted to go back the next day. The next morning my mom started me at a new school, Northeast Middle School. I felt so out of place there, so I only stayed five days. Then I started homeschool. Being home all the time was miserable. I hated it. Every time I thought about going back to Southern that girl's words played back in my mind. Soon enough I couldn't handle being at home 24/7. On January 28, 2011, I started at Southern again and was so nervous. It was my 14th birthday and I wasn't letting anything bring me down. I finished middle school there and it turned out to be one of the best years of my life. Everything was very positive from the time I returned until the end of the school year.

My first year of high school was a joke to me. I didn't take anything seriously and was too caught up with my friends. I'm smart, but I just wasn't using my brain when I was having fun. I regret that whole year every day now because that brings my overall GPA down. This school year I decided to come to I-LEAD Charter School to have a better learning environment. It was a great decision. I've gotten nothing but As all year and I no longer take school as a joke. This school is one of the best things that has ever happened to me.

I want a lot for myself in the future. I hope to graduate from Hawaii Pacific University with my master's degree in social work or secondary education so I could become a history teacher. If I become a social worker, I want to work with veterans and set up rehabs, and help them get psychological help when it's needed. I want to make enough to live comfortably, but I want to be happy. Helping people makes me happy, especially those who served our country. They took care of us; now it's our turn to take care of them. Honestly as long as my family is happy and living comfortably, I will be completely satisfied with my life.

I am Precious Sewell

soundcloud.com/a-picture-is-worth/precious

Where Do I Come from?

I think it's a pride issue when Hispanics say that they don't talk about their family or history. Some people are willing to share and others keep it to themselves. Either way, you never know if you might inspire someone out there. You never know if people can relate to your story. All you can hope for is that at least one person gets where you are coming from. I have been told things that I can't remember and I remember things that I never told. So here are some of those memories from my perspective.

The Lower East Side is my hometown. I was born there. I went to school there. I don't remember much, but claim Manhattan, New York, because my family has so much history there. My grandmother came from Puerto Rico with her family when she was 15. She tells me stories all the time. Like how the pizza was only 15 cents and how the bodegas used to sell two-liter maltas. She moved into an apartment building on Broom Street and had her family of nine children, my mother being the third-youngest. And it's funny because they all have nicknames. It goes Peter, Mita, Tita, Tati, Tuti, Tony, Titi (my mom), Juny and Papo. Try saying that three times! Long story short, my parents grew up in the same building, so most of my family from both sides know each other. When I go to family reunions on my dad's side, they always say things like, "How's Tati?" and "I heard papo came out of prison." Oh if that building could talk…. What would it say?

My mother and father got married at a young age. They had my brothers, sister and me back to back. I am the third-oldest and the first girl. I am happy with my spot and wouldn't change it for the world. Growing up, one of the things I remember most was when we would go to my tia Tita's house in Staten Island, New York. My uncle had a baseball team and my dad was on it so we would drive out there every single Saturday. It was awesome because my tia has this huge house and it would always feel like home when we would stay over.

My father worked as a truck driver and then at a pickle place where they sold huge pickles. After a while he found work in Pennsylvania. We then moved to the small town of Reading in 1999; I was four then. My father found a job at the Berks County Prison as a correctional officer and my mother took a job at the Northwest Elementary School as an aide. When we first arrived, we moved into this huge house on Douglass Street, where a good number of my other family members lived as well. We were always surrounded by people, always. I never had my own room, never, but I didn't mind because I always had someone to play with. I remember so much in that big house. Like how one time my sister called the police. She came up to me and said "Joc, guess what, I called 9-1-1." I didn't believe her until five minutes later when we got a knock at the door and two police officers were standing there saying, "We got a call." I don't remember what happened to Mariah after that. Or like the time my tooth was loose and my cousin Annette was having a hard time getting it out with the floss, so my tio Juny came and said, "Let me see, I promise I won't do anything to it." I should have never trusted him because, Lord behold, he punched it right out and I couldn't even find it.

Times were good there but my parents wanted to move out and get their own place with just the five of us. We moved right down the street on Clinton. I still remember the address, 653 Clinton Street. I remember my childhood there, too. That is where I first learned how to ride a bike. I grew up a lot in that little house. We never complained about things like the house size. This is where I can relate to *The House on Mango Street*.

My siblings and I went to the school that my mom worked at. I think she really wanted to see and be with us every day, 24-7. I loved elementary school so much. I always say that I wish I was a little kid again because you have no worries. You just live life. I always had honor roll and was so good at my multiplication. I was even in a multiplication contest there, but I lost. I loved the way my teachers taught me. I still, to this day, remember important information from elementary school and apply it to my everyday present life, from manners to grammar.

We lived there for about five or six years and then moved to Antietam Mount Penn, a place in Exeter. My parents got a big house with a backyard. Everything was ours and it felt great. I remember when my mom and dad broke it to my sister and me that we weren't going to have our own room. We were promised that in the previous house but my dad said that my brothers were older and they needed more privacy. It was tight. But the plus side was that we got the attic. It was really big and really pink. I had a walk-in closet. The house was so roomy that sometimes I didn't even know what to do.

When we started school, I was nervous. It was only fourth grade. I remember my teacher Mrs. Lewis. She used to read to us, and always smelled like beer and pretzels. The academics were a challenge that I absolutely loved. I played a few sports for the first time: softball, field hockey and basketball (I was always on the tall side). When I got to the high school, I felt so excited because we were more independent. The food was like hotel food. The classes were awesome. Even chorus was on point.

We moved back to Reading when my parents split up. My mom found a place on Franklin and I went to Southern Middle School for 8th grade. It was a total difference from Antietam. I got used to it though. I went to Reading High for 9th grade and The Citadel for 10th. I came to I-LEAD in 11th and now I'm completing my 12th-grade year. I have learned so much here. I appreciate all of the experi-

ences that I have had here and will apply
 some of them to my life as I
take it one day at a time.
Until then, my life's story
has yet to be continued....

I am Jocelyn Vargas

soundcloud.com/a-picture-is-worth/jocelyn

"Education is the most powerful weapon which you can use to change the world."
—*Nelson Mandela*

Angel's Wings

Pop! And there goes a purple baby. Well, that's what my mom told me when I asked her. She told me I was born with half a lung and I was extremely skinny for a baby. I could have died but guess what I'm still alive. She also told me that my father came at the last minute and that my uncle was there all the time visiting her. If my father had not arrived on time for my birth, I would be named Martinez instead of Ynirio. My name is Angel Gabriel Ynirio Roque Gonzalez.... OK, my name doesn't really have "Gonzalez" in it but I really like it because my uncle is the bomb, he's like a second father to me.

After my birth I just lived in my house in Puerto Rico. Back then I was a really bad kid and very carefree ever since I was 5 months old. It was fun until I had to live in the Dominican Republic with my grandmother and grandfather. Probably because I didn't eat at all, but that doesn't mean she had to send me to another country by myself! I was 3 when my mom sent me to the D.R. It wasn't so bad living there with grandma. She always tried her best to get me to eat something or at least drink something healthy. Grandma soon taught me how to eat or to make things easier to say.

My grandfather *forced* me to eat by smacking me and sticking the spoon in my mouth.

During my time in the D.R., I also learned how to write and read in Spanish for two years. When I was 5, I got in trouble with some chicks and I don't mean girl "chicks" I mean chicken chicks. I started messing with the chicks because they were so small and I picked one up; then it started chirping and bit me or chirped me or whatever. I accidently dropped it and then the mama chicken came to whoop my ass for messing with her baby chick. My grandfather found me being chased by the chicken, so he chased us around and in the end he killed the chicken for us to eat. He then finished what the chicken started, and that's whooping my ass.

After my little country hopping, I left the D.R. and went back to P.R. with my mom and dad, but when I got back, my parents were packed up with everything from our house and they told me we were moving. I asked where and they told me we were going to America. To me back then, America sounded like a cartoon character from Looney Tunes, but turns out it's a country. I always thought that a country was a planet. Yes, I thought countries were planets but that doesn't matter and besides I was a kid back then so don't judge me.

My dad left my mom when I was 5. After that, my mom and I moved to Orlando, Florida, with everything we could carry. We stayed at my uncle's house for a few months before we got our own apartment. At that time I was already in second grade. I was a little bitch at that time. I was bullied by some kids who were a lot smaller than me in height but were older than me in age, so I tried to ignore all the bullying. As a matter of fact, the only reason I started getting bullied was because I was protecting an Asian boy who they were making fun of. Every day those other kids bullied me, but I was always all right because I didn't really care what they did to me.

You know those times in elementary school, that time when you got a first love or crush and, well, I had that. She was my hope and the girl I had my first crush on, Valentina. But the problem is that I never had the balls to tell her how I felt. I always tried to get her attention but it never worked. One day, on a Wednesday, it was recess, so all of the kids in my class left to the park to play all kinds of games. The other classes were also out for recess. The kids that bullied me were also coming out for recess, and they immediately found my

Asian best friend and ran to bully him (well that's what I thought). The bullies started bullying Valentina instead of my best friend. When I saw that, I felt something flare inside me for the first time. I did not know what it was at the time, but I ran up to the bullies and just connected my fists to each of their faces and broke their noses, but it wasn't just that. I also beat them down until someone had to stop me.

After this little connection with the bullies, I got into trouble and my mom wanted to know what happened. I explained it to her. When I was finished, I thought she would be mad at me, though she just thought that it was adorable what I did but didn't want me to fight again. There was more bad luck for me in second grade, but I didn't know what was coming for me.

A few weeks after my little bully problem, I played with a few random kids in my cousin's neighborhood. They were playing with a boomerang that I found very interesting. The kids were throwing the boomerang and catching it like it was a ball. There was no problem at all, and I decided to play with them and mess around with the boomerang. That was the worst decision that I ever made in my childhood. When it was my turn to throw the boomerang, I just mindlessly threw it. I noticed a few seconds after I threw the boomerang that it was coming straight back to me. I didn't know what to do so I just moved my head to the left and then... Bam! It hit me right on my eyebrow. It really hurt but what I didn't notice was the blood dripping until I saw myself in the mirror and busted out crying.

In fifth grade, my mother bought a house for us to live in. We had lots of good memories in that old house. I played baseball in the front of the house, and one time I got into trouble. I broke the window to our neighbor's house with a stick and rock, and just like that a perfect base hit, but the consequence was a good beating by mom, which very much hurt me as much as it hurt her. I also had two new best friends, Brittany and Willie.

It was very different in sixth grade. I didn't have many friends and was not "popular" like some of the kids there. Brittany and Willie fit in great with them but I didn't. A lot of the popular kids really pissed me off during sixth grade with their bull.

I had to move again with my mom because she couldn't pay the bills for our house. She gave me the decision to move to Reading, PA, or go to Texas with her boyfriend. I decided to go back to Reading with her. I had no problem at all back then, but that was because I was thinking about myself. My mom was always 100% with me, willing to do everything for her "little boy" and I never even thought about how my mom felt. When I got to Reading I started seventh grade at Northeast Middle School, where I was at first a little shy.

I am Angel Ynirio

soundcloud.com/a-picture-is-worth/angel

AFTERWORD

This book is part of a shared social enterprise now scaling across the nation. The concept is simple: Schools join the program, receive professional-development training and then launch their own *a picture is worth...* program.

Students participating in each school then submit their portraits and essays to the initiative for inclusion in future editions of *a picture is worth....* A team drawn from each participating school across the nation then selects up to 25 essays and photos for print and digital publication. Schools purchase each new edition as the program expands, developing additional resources for its evolution. All participating schools and students have their work featured on the project's national website.

Working together, we actively help future generations of youth tell their stories and master essay writing in the process, all while achieving critical components of the Common Core curriculum related to language and literacy competencies.

To find out how to engage as a student, teacher or school leader, visit us at www.apictureisworth.org and click the community link.

Every learner in each school has a unique and precious soul that holds an important story within, one still being written into the book of time that deserves a patient and nurturing audience. If, as Maya Angelou wrote, there is no greater agony than bearing an untold story, there is also no greater joy than its birth.

David Castro
Alisa del Tufo